LEADERSHIP

the challenge for the
information profession

Sue Roberts and Jennifer Rowley

facet publish

D0294514

Published by
Facet Publishing
7 Ridgmount Street
London WC1E 7AE
www.facetpublishing.co.uk

Facet Publishing is wholly owned by CILIP: the
Chartered Institute of Library and Information
Professionals.

British Library Cataloguing in Publication Data
A catalogue record for this book is available
from the British Library.

ISBN 978-1-85604-609-1

First published 2008

Typeset from authors' disk in 10.5/15 pt
Original Garamond and Futura by Facet
Publishing.
Printed and made in Great Britain by MPG
Books Ltd, Bodmin, Cornwall.

Contents

Introduction

This book offers an open invitation to all professionals and aspiring professionals in information management to reflect on and engage with the development of their leadership role and contribution. Our underlying assumption is that leadership is beneficial at all levels of an organization, and has both internal and external facets. Leadership is relevant for a wide range of roles and can take a number of different guises. Leadership development involves developing capacity to provide leadership in a range of different contexts. It includes developing the leader's own capacity, as well as acting as a catalyst, facilitator and coach to others in the development of their leadership potential.

Leadership capacity is required at all levels of the information profession. Within the information profession there are concerns about the availability and development of top leaders who may provide leadership to significant library and information services, and commercial concerns in the information industry, and in addition shape their community's vision in relation to the importance of a professional and well-informed approach to information and knowledge policy and strategy. There is also concern about leadership capacity within information services. Professional staff, without necessarily having a formal management role, may be called on to lead an interdisciplinary team in aspects of its development of digital citizenship or e-learning, or they may have a supervisory role in relation to tasks or a small group of individuals. All of these roles require leadership, and demand that individuals develop their leadership capacity.

Just in case you are thinking that leadership is not for you, we urge you to linger a little longer. Not all leaders recognize that they aspire to be leaders. Some leaders are driven by more specific agendas. They may want to be a good and successful manager. They may have a drive to make a difference. Alternatively, they may enjoy change and learning. These orientations may inadvertently place them in leadership roles; they may be surprised to find that others are following them, but when this happens in order to take forward their agenda they have to be prepared to accept the responsibility for their followers and take up the mantle of leadership. Others aspire to leadership because they welcome the opportunity to develop and inspire other people or because they welcome the status, control and power that they perceive to be associated with leadership.

Leadership is a complex phenomenon, which is executed in different ways by different people in different contexts. This book uses theoretical concepts and models, coupled with practical tools to encourage reflection and evaluation in support of leadership development. Theory and reflection alone do not automatically lead to enhanced leadership capacity, but they are important ingredients. Our objective is to offer a set of concepts and models which will support you in thinking about and developing your own approach to leadership. No other book offers such a comprehensive and topical perspective on leadership in the context of information services and the wider information industry. In this book we have tried to offer a more sophisticated digest of ideas on leadership for information professionals, and by so doing lay down the gauntlet to invite other practitioners and academics to continue the dialogue around leadership in information organizations.

This book is designed as a companion volume to the widely acclaimed *Managing Information Services* (2004) from the same authors. One chapter of that text addressed management *and* leadership; consequently the authors felt there was significant potential in considering leadership further. Leadership shares both philosophical foundations and specific features with this companion work. Both are written by a team that comprises a management academic and a practising information services manager and are grounded on an underpinning philosophy that theory and practice should be tightly intertwined. Theoretical models and concepts have their foundations in practice. The applications of theories and concepts can assist in sense making, communication, sharing and analysis. They can act as frameworks for the articulation and sharing of best practice, and promote shared learning. Such application of theory in its turn advances and develops theory to allow it to accommodate a wider variety of contexts, and to evolve in line with practice.

The style throughout is one of enquiry rather than instruction. Not only do we not believe that there are universal guidelines to 'how to be a good leader', but it would be very arrogant of us to suggest that we had the answers in such an important area. We are, however, fascinated by leadership, and in particular its many facets in the context of the information profession, and want to share some of our journey towards a better understanding of leadership.

The first chapter provides orientation by discussing issues such as the importance of leadership for information management, the difference between leadership and management, and the imperative of change. The next two chapters discuss different aspects of leadership. Both are strongly grounded in theoretical perspectives on the nature and execution of leadership. Chapter 2 encourages the reader to think about and evaluate themselves as a leader through introducing topics such as leadership traits and styles, emotional intelligence, values, gender, communication styles and personality. Chapter 3 moves on to examine leadership in context, taking into its scope contingency theories and transformational theories of leadership.

The remaining chapters pick up key aspects of leadership roles. Chapter 4 draws on a number of different literatures and perspectives to explore approaches to promoting change and innovation. Chapter 5 focuses specifically on the 'people' aspects of leadership, addressing themes such as team-building and development in a range of different kinds of team situations, plus concepts of empowerment and followership. Chapter 6 takes forward one very important role of the leader, visioning and setting direction, through mission statements, policies, values and culture. Chapter 7 reviews the potential strategies for leadership development for individuals and others with whom they are working. It introduces and encourages evaluation of leadership programmes and leadership initiatives in the information management profession. Finally, Chapter 8 explores the role of the information professional in leading and influencing in contexts where the other stakeholders are not information professionals. This involves understanding and capitalizing on the leadership, management and information competences that working in an information service or information industry environment develops. Each chapter draws extensively on examples from library and information services, discussing issues and scenarios from across the sectors.

Bland generalizations and dry theory would not communicate the reality. We have therefore used examples and cameos to tell the story and provide ideas for reflection. A number of the features listed below are suitable for use in either individual reflection and learning or in group learning situations, such as professional education, training courses and seminars. Although the specifics of some of the UK-based illustrative examples may not be internationally applicable, the drivers, issues and approaches are widely shared.

The book features:

1 *Learning objectives* Study objectives are identified at the beginning of each chapter.

2 *Summaries* Summaries review the content of each chapter and draw together the key themes that have been developed.

3 *Reflections* Reflection points are distributed throughout each chapter. These questions are intended to encourage readers to pause and think about the text. They can also be used as group discussion points.

4 *Review questions* Review questions appear at the end of each chapter. These are examination-type assessment questions designed to encourage readers to review, interpret and apply the material in the chapter. They provide an opportunity to test retention. The questions also flag the key issues that are addressed in each chapter, and in that sense provide an additional summary of key themes. Although all questions can be answered from the material in this book, better answers will also use illustrations from professional practice and experience, and concepts from wider reading.

5 *Challenges* Each chapter has a list of challenges, which should not be confused with the review questions. The basic concepts for thinking about the review questions are embedded in the text of the respective chapter, but the challenges are designed to provoke further investigation, discussion and debate. There are no easy answers to the challenge questions; they are precisely the imponderable questions that information service leaders and researchers know to be at the heart of

practice and theory, but for which any answers are contingent on context, and likely to change tomorrow.

6   *Case studies* Each chapter includes a case cameo based on interviews with leaders at all levels in information organizations to illustrate further the application and relevance of the concepts in the chapter, and to encourage debate and deliberation. Each case cameo is accompanied by case study questions that can be used as the basis for individual reflection or group discussion.

7   *References and additional reading* Titles cited in the text and other useful sources are listed at the end of each chapter.

Audience

This book is designed for information professionals and aspiring information professionals who are interested in understanding leadership and developing their own leadership practice in the context of information services and the wider information industry. It applies to any sector and would also be valuable as a professional education text.

Acknowledgements

We are grateful to various organizations for permission to reproduce extracts from their document or websites. Acknowledgement is included adjacent to the individual items. We would also like to express our thanks to the team at Facet Publishing whose enthusiasm and encouragement have been invaluable. Once again we thank our families – Steve, Peter, Shula, Zeta and Mark – for their implicit support for this project.

Reference

Roberts, S. and Rowley, J. (2004) *Managing Information Services*, London, Facet Publishing.

1

Context and challenges in leadership

Learning objectives

After reading this chapter you should be able to:

- ☑ appreciate the need for leadership within library and information services
- ☑ understand the relationship between management and leadership
- ☑ engage in the debate about the link between leadership and change
- ☑ engage in the debate surrounding the state of leadership within the library and information profession
- ☑ understand the underpinning philosophy of this book and how the different chapters and elements interconnect
- ☑ begin to consider the approaches and challenges to 'self leadership' and managing yourself.

Introduction

This chapter provides orientation both to the book and to the concept and challenges of leadership. It will discuss issues such as the importance of leadership for information services of all types, provide an overview of the key theories surrounding the relationship between management and leadership, and explore the link between leadership and the imperative for change within organizations. The chapter then discusses the challenges for leadership within library and information services across the sectors and globally, drawing on theory, literature and practice, with illustrative scenarios. The next section provides an insight into the underpinning philosophy of this book and our approach to considering leadership for 21st-century information services; this signposts themes in future chapters and interlinks topics in a holistic way. Finally, the chapter highlights the critical importance of 'self-leadership', which is a recurrent theme. We hope this will initiate or strengthen the self-reflection that is required by all leaders at whatever stage of their career and personal and professional development.

Why leadership?

In *Managing Information Services* (Roberts and Rowley, 2004) we explored leadership briefly as one aspect of a chapter called 'Management and leadership'. We rapidly realized that leadership as a concept – the theories, myths and practices surrounding it – was fundamental to the present and future development of library and information services across all sectors and all nations. Handy (1993, 96) asks provocatively and ironically, 'Surely a group of intelligent, well-meaning individuals can tackle any problem without the need for a leader?', yet history, research and our own experiences dispute this assumption!

This obsession with leadership pervades all aspects of our lives. Writers on the current state of leadership globally have identified a 'crisis' in leadership at the level of politics and society as well as within organizations (Bennis and Nanus, 1997; Taffinder, 1995). There is a cynicism and scepticism towards political and business leaders that appears to have accelerated as the world becomes more unstable and as change becomes increasingly rapid. As a consequence, 'Try as they might to influence their economies or to engineer change in society, political leaders must know that their capacity to do so is very limited' (Taffinder, 1995, 19), and so they must take on a different role from past leaders who lived and worked in a context of greater certainty.

Over the past decade, writers have bemoaned the 'death of leadership', asking 'Has leadership failed? Or worse, is it simply absent?' (Walsh, 1994,

24). As Bennis and Nanus (1997, 1) lament, 'Everybody agrees that there is less of it than there used to be.' Moreover, the vast number of theoretical books and self-help books on leadership and its development (and their popularity!) demonstrate that there is still a very real need for leadership in society and organizations. This becomes even more significant when we consider the 'megatrends' that we will experience during our personal and working lives. Naisbitt (Bennis and Nanus, 1997) presents these changes as a paradigm shift, represented in Table 1.1.

Table 1.1 Naisbitt's megatrends (from Bennis and Nanus, 1997)

From	To
Industrial society	Information society
Forced technology	High tech/high touch
National economy	World economy
Short term	Long term
Centralization	Decentralization
Institutional help	Self-help
Representative democracy	Participatory democracy
Hierarchies	Networking
North	South
Either/Or	Multiple options

We can all identify with different aspects of these trends, for example the reality of working in a world economy with global repercussions rather than on a local scale. All of these trends can also be interpreted from a library and information services perspective and this will be further explored later in this chapter.

REFLECTION Consider the trends in Table 1.1 and their impact on your life. Are there any that are particularly relevant to you?

The literature gives us the impression that society needs leaders to help steer us through challenges and uncertainties, and to provide direction and meaning. If leadership is seen to be missing from 21st-century society, and if the current challenges are so great, what do we actually need and want from our leaders? Consideration of this question clarifies why leadership is so important and can be so powerful within organizations and contributes to the discussion of the nature of leadership and leaders. Kouzes and Posner (2003) investigated the expectations that 'followers' have of leaders and developed a table charting the characteristics of superior leaders. This is represented in Table 1.2.

Table 1.2 Characteristics of superior leaders (Kouzes and Posner, 2003)

Characteristics (in ranked order)	Percentage of managers selecting (from 2,615)
Honest	83
Competent	67
Forward-looking	62
Inspiring	58
Intelligent	43
Fair-minded	40
Broad-minded	37
Straightforward	34
Imaginative	34
Dependable	33
Supportive	32
Courageous	27
Caring	26
Co-operative	25
Mature	23
Ambitious	21
Determined	20
Self-controlled	13
Loyal	11
Independent	10

From Table 1.2 the characteristics of superior leaders can be identified as honesty, competency, and being forward thinking (visionary) and inspiring – a mix of personal attributes and values, and specific skills. Another view of what 'followers' want from their leaders from Goffee and Jones (2001) can be summarized as: significance (to feel valued), community (to feel part of something) and excitement (to feel challenged). Both views emphasize that leadership is a very personal thing and is based on relationships between people.

Finally, to the questions 'Why leadership?' and 'What do people want from leaders?' we should also add, 'What is effective leadership?' To illustrate the importance of effectiveness we need only look at where leadership has transformed an organization or inspired a group of people to do extraordinary things and conversely where it has had a negative impact. At this stage, we would simply point out that effective leaders are involved in:

◆ creating, sharing and communicating vision
◆ shaping culture
◆ developing the potential of others
◆ connecting with people and building successful relationships
◆ taking a holistic and wider perspective.

REFLECTION Think about a positive experience you have had of a boss or colleague providing leadership. What did they do that had such a positive impact?

The relationship between leadership and management

It is important to contextualize approaches to leadership and its development within the current theory and thinking on leadership and management, particularly as there is often confusion between the two. The study of leadership is a relatively recent discipline and writers have discussed and argued extensively over the distinction between leadership and management. Most agree that there *is* a distinction, summarized by us (Roberts and Rowley, 2004) as:

Managers – internally focused, will complete the task; operators, problem-solvers

Leaders – externally focused, have vision; strategists, catalysts, looking to the future

Management – concerned with what people with responsibility for others actually *do*

Leadership – ability of people to *influence* others towards achievement of goals

Such distinctions are felt by some people to be unhelpful, as they can be viewed as portraying leadership as positive and management as negative. In addition, some authors view the two concepts and roles as mutually exclusive – one person cannot be both as they have incompatible values. However, Yukl (2002) argues convincingly that, although management and leadership are distinct processes, and people can lead without being a manager and can manage without being a leader, they are interlinked, as leadership is an essential management role that pervades other roles. Writers also stress the value of effective management and feel strongly that it should not be denigrated as a function. It is useful to consider the *scope of leadership processes*, which highlight the extent of influence that leadership can have. This can be summarized (Yukl, 2002, 7) in terms of a leader's sphere of influence over:

◆ the interpretation of external events by members
◆ the choice of objectives and strategies to pursue
◆ the motivation of members to achieve the objectives
◆ the mutual trust and co-operation of members
◆ the organization of work activities
◆ the development of member skills and confidence
◆ the learning and sharing of new knowledge by members
◆ the enlistment of support and co-operation from outsiders.

It is important to stress that leadership is complex. To get to grips with it and reflect on our own leadership abilities and potential – and those of others – we must not simply look at the characteristics and actions of the individual but consider it within the context of organizations and in particular what organizations require in terms of leadership at different stages in their development. For example, during a financial crisis, an organization may require directional and strong leadership; but during a period of rapid change and growth, a leader may need to encourage participation and empowerment among their staff. As Taffinder (1995, 38) summarizes, 'It means that it is part of the wider environment of business.' This is explored in considerable detail throughout this book with specific contextual examples provided, particularly in Chapter 3, 'Leadership in context'.

REFLECTION Can you think of different instances and contexts when leaders behaved in different ways? Can you see why they took different approaches?

Conceptions of 21st-century leadership

The whole of this book centres around exploring conceptions of leadership and how they can be applied within the 21st-century information management context. As Chapter 2 illustrates, there are multiple theories of leadership traits and styles that can be adopted, adapted or rejected. In this contextualizing chapter, it is important to stress that leadership is 'slippery', meaning different things to different people, and must be viewed flexibly. This sense of *adaptive* leadership pervades the book and is itself a feature of current notions on leadership.

It may be useful to consider briefly at this point *How do we conceive of 21st-century leadership?* There remain tensions in modern concepts of leadership with the 'new leader' still seen as a visionary, charismatic individual, seemingly at odds with the concept of the 'superleader' who aims to develop leadership at all levels of the organization. Authors are certainly now more critical of the 'larger than life' leader who leads from the front, seeing effective leadership as a process created by an individual (the 'learning leader') rather than dependent on their personal qualities (Hooper and Potter, 2001). There is a definite de-emphasis of control in new leadership models, revealing a shift towards participative management and distributed leadership where staff at all levels are empowered in their roles.

Leadership and change

Many authors make the intrinsic link between leadership and change; this is evident in the generic leadership literature and more specifically in information services literature – 'There is no doubt that all activity towards change and transformation of services always refers to the importance of good and strong leadership' (Gent and Kempster, 2002, 53). Moreover, it is recognized that the 'task of leading such services has changed beyond recognition' (Corrall, introduction to Parsons, 2004), with constant change the norm rather than the exception.

Chapter 4 explores in detail the role of leadership in promoting change, innovation and creativity within a dynamic environment. At this stage we would like to stress that we agree with Hooper and Potter (2001, 6), who see leadership as all about 'the increasing challenge of change'. Consequently effective leaders have to 'thrive on chaos' and move from the 'comfortable' to the 'uncomfortable.' Kouzes and Posner (2003) also support this view, arguing that an effective leader must challenge the status quo, seek out opportunities and constantly look to engender a climate that embraces change.

REFLECTION How easy is it to 'thrive on chaos'? How could you prepare yourself for this?

Leadership in library and information services

As highlighted in the introduction to this book, both public and academic library sectors are concerned with leadership, and particularly succession planning for the future. There is also a suggestion in the literature that senior library staff are not necessarily always ready for leadership. In the public library sector, research undertaken by Mullins (2005) into the perceptions of senior managers indicates an apparent lack of understanding of the distinction between management and leadership. Moreover, he concludes that leadership qualities are scarce, with senior managers focusing too much on 'library' skills and not enough on leadership. Both Mullins (2005) and O'Connor (2007) suggest that the library and information profession has been too 'narrow', too focused on 'the ordinary and the mundane', and that staff need to consider the intelligences that they require to pursue their work and lives, and to succeed as leaders. Consequently, if there is to be significant change in perceptions on library leadership and the attributes and behaviours needed for the future, we will require a 'mental shift'.

A project undertaken in UK higher education institutions, led by Birmingham University, explored recruitment, training and succession planning issues for heads of information services. Challenges identified included obstacles to recruitment, skills gaps, training and development needs, the increased pace of change for managers and the increase in hybrid roles that encompassed diverse services, not simply libraries. The key management skills found to be lacking were:

- strategic management and leadership
- ability to manage change
- customer focus-orientation.

It should also be stressed that leadership is a concern right across library organizations, required in all levels and functions, as 'the development of leadership throughout the organization is the only way to succeed' (Gent and Kempster, 2002). Eastell (2003) also highlights this non-hierarchical approach in a public library context, 'It's much less about finding the next head of library service and far more about finding ways of offering library staff at all levels the opportunity to demonstrate and develop their leadership skills.'

Succession planning for leadership is also a key concern as highlighted by Noon (2004). There is an implicit sense in some authors' work that library and information professionals are reluctant to become leaders, not seeing this as their domain but rather preferring to focus on 'professional' library issues. O'Connor (2007) has even made the contentious suggestion that perhaps professional librarians are not the best people to act as leaders within their profession because they potentially lack a wider, strategic view and the necessary skills and perspective. There are examples of individuals from outside the library profession being recruited to leadership positions, for example corporate IT directors who have been recruited to lead converged IT and library services in the academic sector.

REFLECTION What would be the advantages and disadvantages of having leaders who did not have a library and information background?

This brief review of the literature appears to indicate that the nurturing of leadership potential within the library and information profession is a key priority globally, nationally and locally. Consequently, we can conclude that the leadership shortage and the lack of confidence in leaders in library and information services is very real.

The challenges for leaders in information services

As highlighted earlier in this chapter, we are in the midst of a period of rapid and disruptive change. These broad societal trends are evident in the changes and challenges facing library and information services. The information landscape is changing beyond all recognition as a result of these broader trends, which require a change in thinking in terms of the role of libraries. Eric von Hippel (2006) captures one aspect of this – the shift of power to the user:

> When I say that innovation is being democratised, I mean that users of
> products and services – both firms and individuals – are increasingly able to
> innovate for themselves . . . . Users that innovate can develop exactly what they
> want, rather than relying on manufacturers to act as their (often very
> imperfect) agents. Moreover, individual users do not have to develop everything
> they need on their own: they can benefit from innovations developed and freely
> shared by others.

Taking von Hippel's vision – and the views of other forecasters – libraries must consider what this shift of power, control and authority means for them.

An additional challenge is the sense of an unknown and fragmented future. As O'Connor states, 'The future is often not continuous with or in a linear relationship to the present or the past. We do not have only one future; we have many and we are, in our personal lives, constantly choosing between them. Organisations are the same; they are not what they were; they will not be the same into the future' (2007, 69).

REFLECTION Can you identify several key challenges facing a library service that you know well?

Given the context outlined here, the challenges facing leaders in the 21st-century library and information sector could appear overwhelming. From the perspective of senior leaders who are managing large and complex library and information services, the difficulties, from the strategic to the detailed and day-to-day, can be summarized as:

◆ lack of adequate resources and staffing levels
◆ the amount of bureaucracy, regulation and administration
◆ lack of continuity
◆ time pressures related to workload
◆ poor organizational communication
◆ perception of the library within the wider organization
◆ self-doubt and lack of self-confidence
◆ negative cultures
◆ speed of change and the amount of 'unknowns'
◆ lack of strategic drive and vision.

(After Mullins' research into public library leaders, 2005).

The focus in the library literature does appear to be on the negative aspects of leadership – the barriers to progress, the professional and personal difficulties. Turning this on its head, what could be identified as the positives that would motivate leaders and aspiring leaders? We would summarize these as:

◆ the ability to influence people and organizations
◆ the potential to make a difference
◆ self-development – stretching yourself and testing your skills and abilities in a challenging context
◆ inspiring other staff and seeing them develop
◆ developing services that users really want and need
◆ personal satisfaction.

REFLECTION What other disadvantages and advantages do you see for leaders working within a context characterized by continuous change?

In assessing the challenges for leaders of information services, it is useful to consider some of the more recent challenges facing different sectors and types of services. It is also important to consider how leadership, at all levels, can contribute to overcoming such challenges and what kind of leadership individuals can provide (both in terms of management and non-management positions). This is depicted in Table 1.3.

Table 1.3 Examples of recent challenges and possible leadership roles

Type of library and information service	Nature of challenge scenario	Leadership
Public library	Introduction by public library authority of service standards that at first sight appear bureaucratic and impossible to achieve	Head of Library Service – outline why they must address the standards Customer services staff – champion the service standards Library assistants – think about how to promote them to customers and how to communicate
Academic library	Development of e-learning by the university; the library is not viewed as a partner in this and appears to be being bypassed	Subject liaison librarians – discuss how they could contribute with the departments they liaise with Academic support manager – develops a policy around how they will support e-learning and raises this at departmental meetings
Health service library	Implementation of new role review scheme and pay model that makes staff feel very insecure and concerned about the future	Manager with responsibility for HR issues – provides briefings for staff to demystify the scheme Library assistants – first staff to go through the scheme speak positively to colleagues about the process and the outcomes
Branch library	Rationalization of services as a result of budget cuts may result in the branch closing	Head of library service – goes to meet staff at the branch regularly to discuss their concerns and ensure they are fully involved in the decision-making process Team at the branch library (at all levels) – suggest alternative ways forward

It is clear that leadership is not necessarily always aligned to the management hierarchy and nor should it be. Leadership is not the realm of the most senior staff nor the most experienced, nor the youngest, who are often viewed as the most innovative. The aim is to cultivate leadership at all levels and to recognize it in all types of individuals and roles.

A final challenge for leadership has been described by Yukl (2002) as 'ethical leadership', the sense of moral duty and leadership with a 'higher purpose'. This relates directly to a leader's values and integrity, strongly emphasized by Hooper and Potter (2001) as fundamental to leading in a changing environment. Leaders with a strong ethical driver would therefore consider issues such as equity (in access to services for their customers), inclusion (involving all levels and types of staff in decision-making) and impact (the effect of decisions on stakeholders or the environment).

REFLECTION Give some examples of how a strong ethical stance might influence leadership behaviour.

Self-leadership and management

Given that the challenge of leadership is described as like the 'quest for the holy grail' (Handy, 1993, 97), how can we as individuals improve and develop our leadership abilities at all stages of our career? Although this is covered in detail in Chapter 2, 'Knowing Yourself as a Leader', and Chapter 7, 'Leadership Development', we will consider at this point the 'self' as part of the leadership challenge. The first step is self-reflection, looking to yourself and your own experience, not simply books and theories! 'Look back upon your own experience. You have been both a leader and led by others. What do you think makes a person a leader?' (Adair, 2003, 7). It is hoped that with self-reflection comes self-awareness and self-knowledge, viewed by many current theorists and leadership development authors as the key to unlocking leadership potential and understanding your impact on others.

Can everyone be a leader?

There are two schools of thought with regard to this tricky question. One argues that everyone has leadership potential; this can be nurtured and can come with self-analysis but does also depend on the context within which an individual is working. As stated throughout this book, leadership is not simply something that 'senior managers do' but should be evident through all levels of an organization and also in someone's personal life. Others argue that not everyone can become a leader and that the transition from manager to leader is neither automatic nor easy:

> Most managers, with or without self-analysis, never cross the gulf. I have no truck with organizations which claim that everyone in them is a leader. The vast majority of staff and managers do not lead; call them leaders if you like, but don't expect them to lead. They won't. They can't. (Taffinder, 1995, 42)

The other question to consider is whether you *want* to be a leader, whether you have the desire or the potential. This book aims to provide theories, frameworks, practical examples and inspiration to help develop that potential but it is worth reflecting on whether this is the challenge you wish to take. Taffinder (1995) again provides an extensive questionnaire to help us consider this; we have adapted and summarized it in Figure 1.1.

---

1. **Imposing context**
   Can you stand outside your own organization and see it as it really is?
   Do you understand the context of your business and organization?
   Have you articulated the core of what matters to your business, what you stand for?
2. **Risk making, risk taking**
   Are you serving the future of your organization or merely guarding its past?
   Are you willing to make mistakes and take the consequences?
   Do you actively take risks by seeking opportunities?
3. **Unpredictability**
   Are you prepared to experiment?
   Do you create adventure in your organization?
4. **Conviction**
   Do you believe in yourself?
   Are your opinions your own or someone else's?
   Do you thoroughly believe in what you are doing in your organization?
5. **Generating critical mass**
   Can you make what you believe in happen?
   Can/have you convince(d) people of the urgency of the need to change, to grab opportunities?

Figure 1.1 Leadership questionnaire

Drucker (2005) asks other questions to help us to 'build a life of excellence': these can be summarized as:

1   What are my strengths?
2   How do I work?
3   What are my values?
4   Where do I belong?
5   What can I contribute?

With all of these questions it is crucial to ask for feedback from colleagues, friends and family in order to build up a complete and (hopefully) as truthful as possible a picture. This type of exercise has also been presented as the 'reflective best self' (Roberts et al., 2005), which helps individuals both know themselves and play to their strengths. Taylor (2002, 23) goes further to suggest that there is actually a formula for success in leadership at whatever stage of our lives and careers:

1   Know where you want to go – dream bigger dreams, and know when they have been achieved.
2   Know where you are now – take ownership of your life, and be honest about where you are.
3   Know what you have to do, to get where you want to go – widen your choices, and make true decisions, closing off all other options.
4   Do it! – with a persistent action – persistence is incompatible with failure.

Chapter 2 takes this theme of self-awareness and leadership styles and explores them in much more detail and with many more theoretical models.

REFLECTION Apply Taylor's four-point formula to where you are currently in you career and your life. How useful is it?

The philosophy of this book

We hope that by now the philosophy of this book is beginning to emerge and make sense to you. We would summarize it as follows:

◆   Leadership should be carried out at all levels in an organization – it is not the domain of senior staff only; individuals should consider what leadership role they can play at any level to influence practice.

◆ There is no one best form of leadership for library and information services – leadership needs to be adaptive, flexible and context specific.

◆ Theory and practice must go together and leaders must engage in both – this is the basic approach of this book.

◆ Learning must be at the heart of what we do and we must spend time on leadership development from the start of our careers and at whatever stage we are at – at whatever level, leaders should be striving to improve practice and to learn from others.

◆ We must think about how individuals can improve, develop and deploy their leadership abilities – this requires a commitment from all individuals to their own development.

Figure 1.2 summarizes the key elements of leadership as discussed in this book. We introduce this simple model because it provides a useful benchmark against which to measure the scope and emphasis of some of the theories of leadership and leadership development that are discussed later in the book. The model emphasizes the fundamental importance of people and relationships at all levels, a view that will be built on throughout this book.

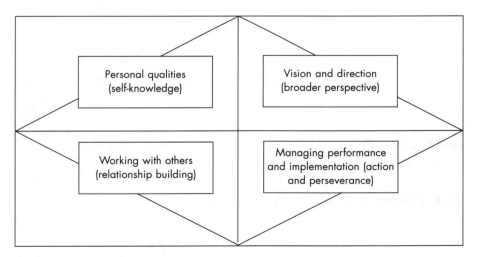

Figure 1.2 Roberts and Rowley's leadership diamond

Summary and conclusions

This chapter has considered the leadership challenge in the 21st century from a broad perspective and then narrowed down to consider the specific challenges for library and information professionals. These challenges are very real and raise questions about the future of the profession if leadership is not seen as central to library and information services staff roles and future development. This chapter has also explored several topics briefly that will be explored in detail throughout this book, for example knowing yourself as a leader, influencing change, and leadership at all levels. It has also attempted to define leadership and its relationship to management.

To conclude, the leadership journey we each undertake is a personal one and we must consider leadership in different ways at different points in our career and life. Taylor (2002, 16) represents this as seven journeys – leadership of:

◆ self
◆ people
◆ teams
◆ company
◆ culture
◆ skills
◆ career.

This book touches on all of these journeys and provides in-depth insight into theories and practice to enable library and information professionals to reflect on where they are and what tools they should use to support their leadership behaviour and development.

Review questions

1   Why is leadership so important to society in general and to the library and information profession specifically?
2   What are the top five characteristics of leaders that 'followers' have identified?
3   How would you define the relationship between management and leadership?

4 Is leadership something that comes only with senior management roles?

5 How would you summarize the difficulties associated with being a senior leader in library and information services?

6 Why is self-awareness seen as so key to successful leadership?

Challenges

1 Why are we (in the 21st century) obsessed with leadership and its development?

2 Has there been a failure of leadership in society?

3 What does an effective leader do?

4 Why are conceptions of leadership so slippery and contested?

5 Are the challenges for leadership within the library and information services common across all sectors?

6 How can self-awareness be cultivated to support effective leadership development and behaviours?

Case study interview with Julia Glynn, Librarian and Technology Consultant, Kenyon College, Ohio, USA

Biography

Julia Glynn currently works at Kenyon College (Gambier, Ohio, USA) as a librarian and technology consultant, and co-manager of HelpLine. Librarian and technology consultants are unique in the library and information science profession. She manages collection development for assigned academic departments, provides reference services, teaches bibliographic and technology instruction sessions, and provides desktop computing and instructional technology support. As the co-manager of HelpLine, Julia oversees the day-to-day running of the desk and manages 20+ student employees. In 2003, Julia graduated with a MS (Master of Science degree) from the University of Illinois' Graduate School of Library and Information Science. She is active in the American Library Association's (ALA's) Intellectual Freedom Round Table, ALA's International Relations Round Table and the Academic Library Association of Ohio.

1 What do you think the major challenges are for the library and information sectors?

Many experienced librarians and library administrators will soon reach retirement age, so the library and information science profession needs to be sure there are enough qualified librarians to fill in these potential employment gaps. Information technology is progressing at a rapid rate and communication methods are quickly evolving, therefore we need to be sure that librarians are properly trained to use, manage and train others to use these new and changing technologies effectively. Multicultural awareness is important as our local communities expand in size and diversity. Library administrators must be smart about purchases as budgets get tighter and costs of materials (print and electronic) increase.

2 What role does leadership have in addressing these challenges?

Current leaders need to be sure that the future leaders are properly trained over the next few decades. Without effective leaders, the profession will flounder as these challenges grow and new challenges develop.

3 How would you describe the difficulties of being a leader (from your own experiences)?

Being a leader is a complex and demanding responsibility. And at certain moments it can be frightening! Even if you don't realize it, someone may be watching to see how you react to a situation. You are a role model whether you want to be one or not. I know that as a manager of my library's computer help desk, my actions reflect not only on me but on everyone who works at the library and the service point. If I lose my cool during a tense interaction with a patron, not only will I lose the respect of my employees, I may also ruin the good reputation of the help desk.

4 How would you describe the benefits?

The best part about leadership is the ability to implement ideas and watch them grow into successful policies. As a relatively new service point manager, I am steadily gaining confidence in how best to run the computer help desk. In the past year, my co-manager and I have created two new positions for experienced student employees who want a higher level of responsibility and redesigned the training process for new student employees. The successes of these ideas encourages me to develop new ones.

5   At what point in your career did you feel, 'I am a leader'?

I'm not sure that I am at the point in my career where I would describe myself as a leader. There are moments when I recognize that colleagues look to me for advice or assistance not because I am a leader but because they see me as more experienced or knowledgeable.

I do feel that I am on my way to being a leader, but someone who still needs to gain more confidence. I have learned to recognize important leadership skills and I work to develop these skills. For example, I am a reluctant public speaker but being an effective communicator is an important skill to have so I continue to place myself in situations which require me to speak to groups of people. Although I still get very nervous, I can feel the improvement in my public speaking skills, and the more I continue to give presentations, the better communicator I will become.

6   What is your approach to 'self-management and leadership'?

My current organization has a flat management hierarchy. Flat organizations tend to have few levels of management between staff and managers, allowing for a workplace atmosphere which allows staff to have a greater level of input in making decisions. In Kenyon's Library and Information Services, this means that we have one vice-president, four directors and then everyone else. By having only a few managers and administrators, this allows everyone the opportunity to be leaders in a variety of areas. Anyone can be a leader for an internal organizational team or choose to run a project on one's own. We are encouraged to be self-managers. No one stands over our shoulders and tells us what to do.

Our flat organization has allowed me the opportunity to try different professional roles and activities. I enjoy this freedom. It can be difficult at first to self-manage. Once I realized the potential of being able to do almost anything within reason, I also realized that I need to manage my time responsibly otherwise I would overwhelm myself and never finish any projects.

7   What does leadership mean to you?

This is a tough question. A leader is not necessarily a manager or an administrator, but rather someone whom colleagues gravitate towards out of professional respect. Some people aim to be leaders, others have the role thrust upon them by other people.

My ideal leader is someone who is professionally accomplished, trustworthy, self-aware but also able to see the world through the eyes of others, and a 'big picture' thinker.

References and additional reading

Adair, J. (2003) *Not Bosses but Leaders*, 3rd edn, with P. Reed, London, Kogan Page.

Bennis, W. and Nanus, B. (1997) *Leaders: strategies for taking charge*, 2nd edn, London, HarperBusiness.

Drucker, P. (2005) Managing Oneself, *Harvard Business Review*, (January), 1–12.

Eastell, C. (2003) The Key to Ciara and the Next Generation of Public Library Leaders, *Library + Information Update*, (April), 40–1.

Gent, R. and Kempster, G. (2002) Leadership and Management. In Melling, M. and Little, J. (eds), *Building a Successful Customer-service Culture: a guide for library and information managers*, London, Facet Publishing, 53–73.

Goffee, R. and Jones, G. (2001) Followership: it's personal too, *Harvard Business Review on Breakthrough Leadership*, Boston, Harvard Business School Press.

Handy, C. (1993) *Understanding Organisations*, 4th edn, London, Penguin Books.

Hooper, A. and Potter, J. (2001) *Intelligent Leadership: creating a passion for change*, London, Random House Business Books.

Kouzes, J. M. and Posner, B. Z. (2003) *Credibility: how leaders gain and lose it, why people demand it*, San Francisco, Jossy-Bass.

Mullins, J. (2005) Are Public Libraries Led or Managed?, *Library Review*, **55** (4), 237–48.

Noon, P. (2004) Developing the Academic Library Managers of the Future. In Oldroyd, M. (ed.), *Developing Academic Library Staff for Future Success*, London, Facet Publishing, 41–60.

O'Connor, S. (2007) The Heretical Library Manager for the Future, *Library Management*, **28** (1–2), 62–71.

Parsons, F. (ed.) (2004) *Recruitment, Training and Succession Planning in the*

HE Sector: findings from the HIMSS project, Birmingham, University of Birmingham.

Roberts, L. M., Spreitzer, G., Dutton, J., Quinn, R., Heaphy, E. and Barker, B. (2005) How to Play to Your Strengths, *Harvard Business Review*, (January).

Roberts, S. and Rowley, J. (2004) *Managing Information Services*, London, Facet Publishing.

Taffinder, P. (1995) *The New Leaders: achieving corporate transformation through dynamic leadership*, London, Kogan Page.

Taylor, D. (2002) *The Naked Leader*, London, Bantam Books.

von Hippel, E. (2006) *Democratising Innovation*, MIT Press, www.web.mit.edu/evhippel.

Walsh, J. (1994) The Time Global 100, *Time*, 4 December, 24.

Yukl, G. (2002) *Leadership in Organisations*, 5th edn, New Jersey, Prentice Hall.

2

Knowing yourself as a leader

Learning objectives

After reading this chapter you should be able to:

- ☑ describe and reflect on your personality and interpret the consequences for your leadership approach
- ☑ understand and be able to apply the concept of leadership traits to yourself and others
- ☑ understand and be able to apply the concept of leadership styles to yourself and others
- ☑ appreciate the role of communication and impression management to leadership
- ☑ understand the role of emotional intelligence in leading others
- ☑ engage in the debate about the impact of gender on approaches to leadership.

Introduction

This chapter encourages you to think about and evaluate yourself as a leader. By exploring several of the basic leadership concepts and theories it provides you with some tools for describing and analysing your leadership approach.

The chapter starts by considering your personality, arguing that personality has implications for the leadership approaches with which we feel most comfortable, both in terms of adoption of our own leadership style and in terms of the leadership that we prefer from others. The two subsequent sections introduce traditional approaches to discussing leadership using leadership traits and styles. Although some would argue that these approaches are simplistic they are still widely used in popular discussion of leadership and can help us to think about what we mean by leadership. The next sections explore key aspects of leadership approaches including communication and emotional intelligence. Finally the chapter opens the debate on the issue of gender in leadership.

Personality and leadership

Before we can understand the approaches that we and others adopt as leaders it is important to understand leaders and potential leaders as people. Theories about personality are one way of understanding who we are, how to describe ourselves, and recognizing how we differ from others. Personality describes the properties of our behaviour that are stable and enduring and which distinguish us from others. There is a widespread belief that personality is related to job performance and career success.

A number of personality theorists have attempted to create a description of the components and structure of personality. There are two main approaches, those that focus on personality types and those that focus on personality traits.

Personality type theories

Personality type theories generate labels that can be applied to a pattern of personality characteristics. Such labels are convenient, whatever the pros and cons of summing up a person with a label. Jung was influential in this field, and his work was developed further by and Myers and Briggs. Jung based his types on their psychological preferences for introversion or extraversion, for sensation or intuition, for thinking or feeling, and for judging or perceiving. Myers and Briggs extended this analysis and embedded it in the Myers Briggs

Type Indicator (MBTI), which is widely used in personality assessment. The MBTI rates personal preferences on the four scales:

Introvert – Extravert
Sensing   – Intuiting
Thinking – Feeling
Judging   – Perceiving

This approach assigns each individual to one side or the other of each dimension, thereby creating 16 personality types.

REFLECTIONS Where would you plot yourself on the MBTI scales? Where would you plot a colleague? What does this say about the nature of any potential leadership–followership relationship between the two of you?

More recent work that uses the concept of personality type relates to the way in which we manage stress. There are a wide range of factors in organizations that may provoke stress, including working conditions, job design, management style, working relationships, uncertainties as to the future, and divided loyalties. There is no doubt that some people survive and even flourish in stressful situations more effectively than others. Friedman and Rosenman identified two 'behaviour syndromes' which sought to explain why different people react differently to stress. They propose that there are two personality types, Type A and Type B:

1   Type A personalities are competitive, and have a high need for achievement. They typically work long hours, and undertake large amounts of work, but have a constant feeling of being under time pressure. They work fast and may be impatient and restless. Their hard work and dedication make them valuable in organizations. They will get things done and drive things forward. On the other hand they create stress in themselves and others and may not be very easy to work with. Type A people are more likely to suffer from stress-related illness than Type B people.

2   Type B personalities are less preoccupied with achievement and are
    more able to take time out to enjoy leisure. They are typically
    easygoing and relaxed and work at a steady pace. They are unlikely to
    lack sufficient time. Their patience and relaxed style make Type B
    people easy people to work with, and in many situations they will be
    good managers.

This model is useful for thinking about a key aspect of our personality: the
way in which we engage with and react to stress. Leaders and senior
managers often operate under a lot of stress. Both Type A and Type B personalities need to learn how to manage their response to stress. Type B
personalities may be too relaxed to drive forward change and lead the
organization in complex and dynamic marketplaces; they need to become
more proactive. On the other hand, Type A personalities need to temper
their propensity to set over-ambitious agendas, and to manage their own
stress levels, and the stress that they can potentially generate in others.

REFLECTION Would you prefer to work for or with an extreme Type A or an
extreme Type B manager or leader?

Personality trait theories

The other approach to profiling personality is the trait approach. Traits are
predispositions to behave in a certain way. An individual can be described
using a number of trait labels such as their levels of anxiety, self-esteem,
autonomy and guilt. Eysenck was interested in the dimensions on which
personality differs. Although he also generated personality types, he was
particularly interested to develop clusters of traits that could be used to
describe or profile a given personality type. Table 2.1 shows the trait clusters
for four of Eysenck's types.

REFLECTION Describe yourself in terms of the traits that you think are important
aspects of your personality. If it is helpful, use some of the traits in Eysenck's trait
clusters.

Table 2.1 Four of Eysenck's trait clusters

Extravert	Introvert	Emotionally unstable	Emotionally stable
Activity	Inactivity	Anxiety	Calm
Expressiveness	Inhibition	Guilt	Guilt freedom
Impulsiveness	Control	Hypochondriasis	Sense of health
Irresponsibility	Responsibility	Lack of autonomy	Autonomy
Practicability	Reflectiveness	Low self-esteem	Self-esteem
Risk taking	Carefulness	Obsessiveness	Casualness
Sociability	Unsociability	Unhappiness	Happiness

Eysenck's work was a precursor to Costa and McRae's work, which led to the development of a model that has been very influential in personality profiling, the big five, or OCEAN. The big five are five trait clusters, with six traits under each of five headings. Table 2.2 shows the big five personality trait clusters, together with the labels that are applied to each end of the spectrum that can be applied to each trait cluster. When this approach is used to profile personality, an individual is rated on their position on each of these scales. So an individual might have the score: O–, C–, E+, A+, and N–. This would mean that they were unimaginative and narrow-minded, traits that might suit a job where focus, concentration and attention to detail were important. But as they are also frivolous, irresponsible and disorganized they may not be suitable for detailed work where it is important to get everything right. On the other hand their scores on the final three clusters tend to support each other more effectively, suggesting that this individual is likely to work well with people. This person is gregarious and warm, and straightforward and compliant. Further they are calm, contented and self-assured.

REFLECTION If you feel there is such a thing as an ideal profile, suggest a big five profile for:

◆ a website designer
◆ a public library branch manager
◆ a university librarian.

Table 2.2 The big five personality trait clusters (based on Huczynski and Buchanan, 2007)

Openness	Explorer (O+)	Preserver (O–)
	Creative, open-minded, intellectual	Unimaginative, uninterested, narrow-minded
Conscientiousness	Focused (C+)	Flexible (C–)
	Dutiful, achievement-oriented, self-disciplined	Frivolous, irresponsible, disorganized
Extraversion	Extravert (E+)	Introvert (O–)
	Gregarious, warm, positive	Quiet, reserved, shy
Agreeableness	Adapter (A+)	Challenger (A–)
	Straightforward, compliant, sympathetic	Quarrelsome, oppositional, unfeeling
Neuroticism (or negative emotionality)	Reactive (N+)	Resilient (N–)
	Anxious, depressed, self-conscious	Calm, contented, self-assured

Some limited work has been carried out on the personal qualities or traits that are appropriate for librarians. These include: creativity, having a sense of humour, energy, outgoing nature, self-motivation, and showing evidence of initiative and resourcefulness (Dewey, 1998). Particularly in the library leadership literature it can be difficult to differentiate between what are seen as personal traits and what are viewed as leadership traits. Further discussion of leadership traits for information professionals is offered in the section 'Leadership traits', below.

Self-concept and understanding who we are

Personality theories with their models of traits and types underpin the assessment methods, such as psychometric assessment, that are used to assess people for recruitment and career progression. Most managers will have had their personality assessed using such tools. Although such tools may produce personality profiles of limited relevance and value, and we may agree or disagree with their results, they can be a useful tool to help us reflect on who we think we are, and where appropriate to discuss this with others. They provide us with terms and labels that we can embrace or reject as good descriptors of our personality. They help us to articulate and therefore work with our self-concept.

Our *self-concept* is the way that we view ourselves, or the set of perceptions that we have about ourselves. Mead (1934) suggested that the self-concept has two components:

◆ *I* – the way 'I' see myself – the unique, individual, conscious and impulsive aspects of the individual
◆ *Me* – the way others see 'Me' – the norms and values of society that the individual learns and accepts, or 'internalizes'.

The personal self is concerned with my perceptions, motives and feelings, and 'Me', the social self, is how I appear to others. We tend to strive for some alignment between how we see ourselves and how we think others see us. Our self-concept is important because it not only allows us to think about who we are and how others see us, and thereby to develop an awareness of our strengths and weaknesses, responses and competencies in specific situations, but also impacts on our confidence and self-esteem. Confidence and good self-esteem are essential to leaders.

Since we adapt our self-concept, we adapt our personality slowly over time. We adapt our behaviours as we experience new situations and learn. We adapt as we take on different roles. So, if you do not see yourself as a leader at this point in time, you may surprise yourself when you find yourself taking a leadership role after you have further experience, and in a different context.

Leadership traits

Early in the 20th century researchers believed that if they could identify the personality traits of leaders, or personality markers, they could identify potential leaders. Management of organizations could then be much enhanced by promoting those individuals into leadership or management positions. A key influence was the 'great man theory', which argues that great men (there is no equivalent theory for women) are born leaders, and they emerge to take power regardless of the social, organizational or historical context. Even today some of us believe that leaders are born, whereas others would suggest that leaders are made or can be developed. The latter position is taken by the leadership-style school of thought discussed in the next section. Apart from this dispute over the basic philosophical stance of trait theories, another problem is the lack of agreement on the key traits exhibited by effective leaders. The identification of a 'good' or 'effective' leader is a subjective one. We might argue that since later thinkers have preferred to consider leadership to be context dependent as discussed in the next chapter, this is not surprising. Another problem is that the traits that are proposed are often vague and it can be difficult to operationalize them so that they can be used to identify or assess leaders.

Despite the limitations of trait theories it is useful to include two well-cited examples of work on trait theories. Stewart (1963) generated the following leadership traits from a study based on American executives' views of leadership qualities:

Judgement	Initiative	Integrity
Foresight	Energy	Drive
Human relating skill	Decisiveness	Dependability
Emotional stability	Fairness	Ambition
Dedication	Objectivity	Co-operation

REFLECTION Analyse the match between the traits identified by the personality trait theories and those generated by leadership theorists. On this basis is it possible to identify a set of personality traits that predispose people to be leaders?

A much more recent piece of work is that conducted by the Hay Group for the British National Health Service (Department of Health, 2002). They suggested that effective and outstanding leaders were characterized by the 15 qualities shown in Table 2.3.

Table 2.3 The qualities of effective and outstanding leaders identified by the Hay Group for the British National Health Service

Personal qualities	Setting direction	Delivering the service
Self-belief	Seizing the future	Leading change through people
Self-awareness	Intellectual flexibility	Holding to account
Self-management	Broad scanning	Empowering others
Drive for improvement	Political astuteness	Effective and strategic influencing
Personal integrity	Drive for results	Collaborative working

Covey (1992) uses traits or characteristics in his notion of 'principles centred leadership'. He argues that the extent to which leaders adhere to moral principles determines their success. Principles centred leaders:

◆ are learning oriented
◆ are service oriented
◆ radiate positive energy
◆ believe in other people
◆ lead balanced lives
◆ see life as an adventure
◆ are synergistic and improve situations
◆ exercise (physically, mentally, emotionally and spiritually) for self-renewal.

It is easy to dismiss trait theories, with their roots in the identification of a 'great man' or a 'good leader', but the recent work done for the NHS described above suggests that there is still some interest in understanding what makes a good leader. People find role models extremely useful in fuelling and directing their own development, and they interpret these role models not just in terms of style, but also in terms of traits and characteristics of the individual. The model from the NHS study, for instance, gives us a sense of what leadership is all about, identifying as it does three dimensions of leadership: personal qualities, having vision and direction, and delivering the service. These can be matched with the dimensions in Roberts and Rowley's leadership diamond (Figure 1.2, page 16). On reflection, the category 'delivering the service' is concerned with 'working with others', an aspect that is emphasized further in style theories, especially Likert's systems of leadership. We suggest that the dimension associated with 'delivering the service' might be divided into 'working with and influencing others' and 'managing performance and implementation'.

So far, the discussion has drawn on leadership theories intended to be applicable in a wide range of different contexts, including for social, political and business leaders. Is there anything special about leaders in the information profession? Who are these leaders? And is there anything to be learnt from an analysis of leaders? Below you are invited to reflect further on the question of leaders you have known and the impact that they may have had on you, but first it may be useful to summarize some of the challenges in identifying leaders in the information profession:

1 There is something of a circular debate: we might argue that we need a definition of a leader (implicit or explicit) before we can identify effective leaders.

2 When identifying leaders for a profession we tend to pick out figures who have been important to the profession as a whole, such as Melville Dewey or Maurice Line. This has a number of drawbacks:
— There is a tendency to overlook leaders at various levels in the profession, and to identify people who have been at the top of, or had high visibility in, their profession.
— In identifying such people as leaders, since we often have no personal interactions with them we are acknowledging them for their public actions or their legacy, or in other words privileging the vision and direction dimension of leadership over the other dimensions identifed in Figure 1.2.
— The analysis of leadership is retrospective, and the styles or qualities that might have been suitable in the past may not be the most appropriate for leading into the future.
— Quite a few of these people have retired or are dead, and are not therefore available as role models!

3 It is becoming increasingly difficult to identify the boundaries of the information profession. For example, it would be perfectly possible to argue that Bill Gates (Microsoft) or Tim Berners-Lee (semantic web) are key leaders for the information profession, whether or not they are seen as members of the information profession community.

4 Leadership qualities are not fixed, so that as individuals develop or face different situations they may adopt different leadership styles.

5 The notion of leadership is evolving so that no list of behaviours or traits can be viewed as stable, which makes it difficult to identify leaders.

6 Any one leader may only exhibit certain leadership traits, and not the complete portfolio.

REFLECTION Identify some leaders of the information profession. Why do you see these people as leaders?

Notwithstanding the challenges associated with the identification of an appropriate identification of leadership qualities or behaviours, and in full recognition of the evolutional and changing nature of leadership, Mullins and Linehan (2006) recently conducted a survey in which top level public librarians were asked to comment on the qualities and behaviours required for pubic library leaders. This study demonstrated that there was a universal agreement on the central importance of vision: 'A leader needs to set the overarching vision and values. Leadership is articulating vision' (2006, 136).

Willingness to take risks and try new ventures
Good judgement
Good verbal skills
Understanding the environment
Good decision-making skills
Openness to new ideas
Learning orientation
Awareness of 'what is happening'
Hands-on involvement
Energy
Ability to get on with people, including the public, staff and managers
Political skills
Commitment

Figure 2.1 Attributes for public library leaders (based on Mullins and Linehan, 2006)

Beyond this agreement, however, librarians tended to differ in the range of attributes that they identified; a cumulative list of 60 attributes was compiled from their responses. Some of these attributes are listed in Figure 2.1. This diversity of perspectives may be related to the different geographical constituencies in the sample (USA, UK and Ireland), or may be a result of the limited discussion of leadership and therefore use of its concepts and terminology in the information profession. Mullins and Linehan (2006) go on to outline negative behaviours. These include the leader:

◆ distancing themselves from staff
◆ staying locked in their office

◆ having an autocratic style
◆ exercising power and control
◆ not being willing to delegate.

The further analysis of negative or toxic leadership attributes would perhaps offer further insights into positive leadership behaviours or at the very least the avoidance of disastrous behaviours.

Leadership styles

Another major group of theories of leadership is based on understanding appropriate behaviour patterns for leaders, and developing them in leaders. Instead of seeking leaders on the basis of personality traits, seek them for appropriate leadership styles. According to Mullins, 'Leadership style is the way in which the functions of leadership are carried out, the way in which the managers typically behave towards members of the group' (2005, 291). If appropriate styles and behaviours could be identified future leaders could be taught to exhibit appropriate leadership behaviours. There is, of course, one major difficulty with this approach – the identification of appropriate leadership style.

At the heart of the discussion of leadership style are the two dimensions of leadership behaviour identified by the early work in the Michigan studies (Huczynski and Buchanan, 2007):

◆ *employee-centered behaviour*, focusing on relationships and employee needs
◆ *production or job-centered behaviour*, focusing on getting the job done.

These two elements were further confirmed and developed by the Ohio studies (Huczynski and Buchanan, 2007). These identified two categories of leadership, which they term consideration, and initiating structure. Considerate leaders are relationship and social needs orientated. They are interested in and listen to subordinates; they allow participation in decision making, are friendly and approachable and support subordinates. The leader's behaviour indicates trust, respect, warmth and rapport, and is likely to promote self-esteem and job satisfaction in subordinates. Leaders who initiate structure are task or job-centred. They focus on how things get done, make expectations clear, emphasize deadlines, and expect subordinates to follow instructions. This leadership behaviour emphasizes production, which is likely to lead to higher task performance. An important contribution of the Ohio studies was to identify 'initiating structure' and 'consideration' as two separate dimensions so that a supervisor can score highly on both. However, later work demonstrates that the question of whether a leader can be both task and people oriented remains open for debate.

Table 2.4 Likert's systems of leadership

System 1	System 2
Exploitative autocratic, where the leader: • has no confidence and trust in subordinates • imposes decisions, never delegates • motivates by threat • has little communication and teamwork.	Benevolent authoritative, where the leader: • has superficial, condescending trust in subordinates • imposes decisions, never delegates • motivates by reward • sometimes involves subordinates in solving problems.
System 3 Participative, where the leader: • has incomplete confidence and trust in subordinates • listens to subordinates but controls decision making • motivates by reward and some involvement • uses ideas and opinions of subordinates constructively.	**System 4** Democratic, where the leader: • has complete confidence and trust in subordinates • allows subordinates to make decisions for themselves • motivates by reward for achieving goals set by participants • shares ideas and opinions.

Developing these themes further Likert (1961) proposed four systems of leadership (Table 2.4), suggesting that effective supervisors adopted either system 3 or system 4 or, in other words, that effective leaders take time to build rapport and relationships with their subordinates. This may sound all very obvious but there are occasions, as we shall discuss in the next chapter, when it is difficult for leaders to operate in a participative or democratic style. The ability to operate in either of these styles depends on:

◆ the leader feeling confident that they can trust subordinates – trust is a two-way street
◆ the subordinates having the experience, knowledge and sense of the 'general good' to make an appropriate decision

◆ rewards being available to be used in motivation
◆ an effective team and organizational culture in which ideas and opinions can be shared without adverse political consequences.

In practice, good leaders use different styles depending on circumstances, although they may have a dominant or preferred style.

REFLECTION What measures does your manager take to build rapport with their team? How could this be further improved?

Communication and impression management

Managers spend much of their time in communication. Leaders understand that people are important, and that communication is central to gaining influence, support and co-operation. Through communication, leaders express and clarify their visions and foster participation and motivation. Communication can be viewed as the lubricant used to keep things moving in a team or organization. Therefore leaders need to be conscious of how they communicate, and understand that communication is a two-way process that involves listening as well as talking. Perhaps even more importantly, leaders recognize that what they are and do communicates more persuasively than what they say.

In general, leaders have three key roles in relation to communication:

◆ to establish culture and values relating to communication style and approaches relating to one-to-one communication
◆ to set and communicate direction through plans, policies and public utterances
◆ to establish and manage communication networks.

The extent of involvement in these activities will vary with the position that the leader holds in the organization. Senior managers have significant responsibility for communicating direction, and managing communication networks. At the other end of the spectrum, first-line managers and professionals in non-management roles have significant responsibility for one-to-one communication with staff, customers and users. Effective communication at this level of the organization is key to the experience of staff and customers. Below we discuss some key aspects of the leadership role in relation to communication. The intention here is not to provide a thorough review of communication theories, but rather to encourage reflection on the importance of communication in leadership.

Understanding each other

The basic model of communication processes at the individual level revolves around the transmitter (the person framing and sending the message) and the receiver (the person receiving and interpreting the message). The transmitter of a message has motives, objectives, personality traits, values, biases and prejudices which colour the content and expression of communication. These affect the information that the transmitter chooses to communicate and the form in which it is communicated, a process described as *perceptual filtering*. The receiver also has their own perceptual filters, which are applied in the interpretation of the message, and there is often a gap between the intended message and the received message. Add to this other physical, social and cultural factors (see Table 2.5) that may affect the communication process, and it is not surprising that people interpret the same message differently, and that any communication process has scope for ambiguity and frustration. Feedback, both verbal and non-verbal (e.g. nodding the head), can help the transmitter to understand how the message has been received, and to modify or follow up accordingly.

Table 2.5 Barriers to effective organizational communication

Power differences	People in different levels of the organization have different perspectives, experiences and objectives.
Gender differences	Men and women have different conversational styles; men tend to talk and project themselves more strongly, while women listen and reflect more.
Physical surroundings	Room size and layout, including seating arrangements, affect communication within an office environment and in meetings.
Language	Even with a common working language people with different languages may communicate differently, with problems arising with idioms, jokes and variations in accent and dialect.
Cultural diversity	Expectations and norms about formal and informal communication, through various channels, vary for different cultures.

There are two main categories of communication: verbal and non-verbal. Verbal communication can be either spoken or written. Spoken conversations are important in building relationships. They typically progress through a series of questions and answers or prompts and responses. Different kinds of questions can be used to control the conversation to varying extents. For example, closed questions such as: 'Which organization do you currently work for?', can be used by the questioner to keep control. On the other hand, hypothetical questions, such as 'What problems do you predict if we change the system?', can be used to open up discussion and provoke creative thinking. Conversations are also controlled through the use of various conscious and unconscious verbal and non-verbal signals, which indicate, for example, when one speaker has finished and another person can speak, or whether others agree with the speaker.

REFLECTION The next time you are in a meeting, formal or informal, sit back and study the approaches that different individuals use to control the conversation. What are the controls used by the person who you would identify as playing a leadership role in that meeting or group?

Alongside verbal communication we use a wide range of non-verbal communication. Unless we are aware of our non-verbal communication, there is a danger that our verbal and non-verbal communication may contradict each other, and undermine the clarity, directness and effectiveness of the communication. Non-verbal communication can occur through:

◆ eye behaviour, including where we are looking, and the extent of eye contact with others
◆ facial expressions, such as whether we frown, smile, or look bored or attentive
◆ posture, such as how we stand or sit, and what we are doing with our hands
◆ limb movements (kinesics), referring to hand gestures, nervous movements and whether we stand still or move about
◆ tone and pitch of voice (paralanguage), which has a significant effect on the message; e.g. 'we *could* meet for coffee tomorrow' and 'we

could meet for coffee *tomorrow*' have slightly different meanings because of the different emphases
◆ distance from other people (proxemics), which communicates messages about the relationship between us and others.

REFLECTION Look at yourself in a mirror; what non-verbal messages might someone pick up from the image that you see in front of you?

Impression management

Whether conciously or unconsciously we all engage in impression management; we seek to manipulate the impression or perceptions that others have of us, and thereby to manipulate their behaviour. We put on smart clothes for an interview; we are careful of what we say in a meeting. Impression management is when we control the signals that we send, and deliberately become aware of the cues that others are sending to us. Impression management may include controlling:

◆ what we do and how we do it
◆ what we say and how we say it
◆ the furnishings and arrangement of our offices
◆ our physical appearance including clothes and makeup
◆ non-verbal behaviours such as facial expressions or postures.

Effective impression management gives greater control and influence in social interactions. Conscious impression management might be seen as no more than an extension of an understanding of how others see us. Some would argue that conscious impression management ensures that we provide the correct signals to others, and this causes interactions to run more smoothly. On the other hand, others would argue that impression management means that the leader is not presenting their true self and this reduces trust and generates suspicion. The truth probably lies somewhere between these two extremes. There are many contexts in organizations when leaders and others are required to play a role, such as an interviewer, or the chairperson in a disciplinary proceeding; to play these roles effectively, the individual needs to engage in some level of impression management. Table 2.6 lists strategies for one type of impression management that a leader might exercise: power talking. In addition, the earlier section on verbal and non-verbal communication identifies key communication channels and processes that can be enlisted in impression management.

Table 2.6 Power talking strategies (based on Huczynski and Buchanan, 2007)

Talking positively	Responding positively, being optimistic, seeking creative solutions and looking for the benefits
Giving credit	Describing achievements positively, ignoring or altering shortcomings, praising others for their success
Learning from experience	Seeing potential 'failures' as learning experiences, thinking positive when things are not going well, and focusing on the future
Accepting responsibility	Admitting feelings, accepting responsibility for actions, and managing use of time
Persuading others	Emphasizing benefits, keeping options open, accepting others' ideas
Speaking decisively	Committing to specific targets, extracting detailed information, setting realistic goals, saying what you want to say
Telling the truth	Saying 'no' when necessary

REFLECTION Give some examples of impression management techniques and activities that you think are acceptable and contrast these with examples that are unacceptable.

Communication networks

The effectiveness of communication within an organization has important consequences for motivation and participation. Leaders in senior management positions therefore have a significant responsibility for managing the range of mechanisms that are used to communicate with employees. Typically these involve:

◆ the design of the management structure and chain of command
◆ team meetings and briefings at all levels in the organization

◆ in-house newspapers, magazines and briefing sheets, in print and electronic form
◆ notice boards and bulletin boards
◆ conferences, seminars, awaydays and workshops
◆ annual reports and any summaries for employees
◆ e-mail communication.

In addition many of the other processes embedded in organizational life are also opportunities for communication, such as the appraisal system, mentoring, and attitude and satisfaction surveys.

Most importantly, managers and leaders have a pivotal role in defining the communication climate within the organization. The term *communication climate* refers to the atmosphere in which ideas and information are exchanged. Gibb (1961) suggested there are two extremes: an open, supportive communication climate, and a closed, defensive communication climate. In an open climate people develop self-worth, feel that they can contribute without fear of reprisal, know that their suggestions will be welcome, that mistakes are viewed as learning opportunities, and they feel secure, trusted and confident. In a closed communication climate information is only released when it is in the interests of the sender to do so and the atmosphere of recrimination, secrecy and distrust can make working life unpleasant. It is important, however, to remember that just providing staff with lots of information does not make for an open communication climate. If there is to be a truly open climate, there must be two or multi-way communication, which requires sensitivity and trust. For staff to value communication processes they need to be part of a wider culture which welcomes their participation; communication must be relevant and topical, and managers must be perceived as trustworthy. In the hurly burly of a political organizational environment, in which confidentiality may be necessary and there is not always time to shape and target communication appropriately, this can be easier said than done.

Emotional intelligence

Leadership is a process of social interaction, where the leader's ability to influence the behaviour of their followers can strongly influence behaviour outcomes. Leadership can be viewed as essentially an emotional process in which leaders attempt to evoke emotions in followers and seek to manage their emotional states (Humphrey, 2002). It is increasingly being recognized that it is important for managers to have emotional intelligence (EI) – the ability to identify, integrate and understand and manage their own and other people's feelings. If we understand how people respond or, even better, are likely to respond in a given situation there is potential for influencing their emotions to create more positive outcomes for both the individual and the organization. Goleman (2000), for instance, suggested that emotional intelligence gives an edge in senior and leadership roles, where conventional intelligence and capabilities are assumed. Increased EI can create faster, deeper and more sustained change, and thereby impact on personal and organizational effectiveness. Table 2.7 outlines Goleman's four fundamental capabilities of emotional intelligence.

Table 2.7 Goleman's four fundamental capabilities of emotional intelligence (based on Goleman, 2000)

Self-awareness	Self-management	Social awareness	Social skill
Emotional self-awareness	Self-control	Empathy	Visionary leadership
Acute self-assessment	Trustworthiness	Organizational awareness	Influence
Self-confidence	Conscientiousness	Service orientation	Developing others
	Adaptability		Communication
	Achievement orientation		Change catalyst
	Initiative		Conflict management
			Building bonds
			Teamwork and collaboration

There are a number of studies that examine the relationship between emotional intelligence and other core aspects of leadership. Key to such research are instruments to measure EI, and other variables such as leadership effectiveness, customer satisfaction and team performance. Such research can offer a number of useful perspectives, but as Kerr et al. (2006) suggest there is considerable complexity associated with the interpretation of such research since there are a number of different scales in use to measure EI. Further, some would argue that since leadership cannot be studied as a rigorous scientific phenomenon, but rather it is necessary to evaluate the perspectives of different stakeholder groups and to accommodate changing circumstances, such scales may at best be volatile, and at worst be entirely inappropriate.

Barling, Slater and Kelloway (2000) open the debate about the relationship between emotional intelligence and transformational leadership style, which is viewed as important in today's changing environment (see Chapter 3 for more development of this topic). They suggest the following reasons why individuals with high emotional intelligence might be more likely to use transformational behaviours:

1   Leaders who know and can manage their own emotions, and who display self-control and delay of gratification, could serve as role models for their followers, thereby enhancing followers' trust in and respect for their leaders. This is consistent with one dimension of transformational leadership, idealized influence.
2   By understanding others' emotions, leaders with high emotional intelligence would be able to reconsider the extent to which followers' expectations could be raised, and thereby to exercise inspirational motivations.
3   Emphasis on empathy and the ability to manage relationships may well result in leaders with high emotional intelligence manifesting individual consideration.

Kerr et al. (2006) established that EI is associated with leadership effectiveness. In particular, employee perceptions of supervisor effectiveness are strongly related to the EI of the supervisor. Their research differentiates between Experiential EI, related to perceiving and using emotions, and Reasoning EI, related to understanding and managing emotions. Experiential EI appears to have a much more significant impact than Reasoning EI on subordinates' evaluation of leadership effectiveness. Or, in other words, leaders can know and understand and even predict emotions, but if they do not adopt appropriate behaviours as a result of this knowledge they are not perceived to be effective leaders.

In conclusion, emotional intelligence is a concept that recognizes that emotions and responses to those emotions are at the heart of leadership. Operationalizing the link between leadership and emotions for the purposes of theory building and to inform practice is work in progress, but there is no doubt that leadership or management that neglects to consider emotions fails to capitalize on a rich area for influencing and motivating people.

REFLECTION Inspirational leaders might be said to excite us and thereby to drive us on to accept new challenges and achievements. Identify a situation in which someone inspired and excited you sufficiently that it made a big difference to you, and those around you.

Does gender matter?

Do men and women lead (and manage) differently? In starting to answer this question it is useful to remind ourselves that much management theory and practice has been created by and is owned by men. Leadership theory and commentary assumed that leaders were men. As a result, unfortunately, male leadership style is the embedded norm, and the more pertinent question is 'Are women leaders different from men leaders?' Clearly, if women can be shown to lead differently from men, then whether you are a man or a woman, it is useful to understand the potential impact of gender on your leadership style and those of both genders with whom you interact.

There are a number of difficulties in untangling the relative leadership styles of men and women. In particular, some commentators are wary of debating differences between male and female leadership styles in an environment where gender parity is the dominant ideology. On the other hand others hold the view that it is simplistic to see women and men as leaders as being the same (Oshagbemi and Gill, 2003). So, over the past 20 years, as the numbers of women in management and leadership positions has expanded, there has been a growing body of research on leadership style. This research has made some interesting observations, which may be very helpful in fuelling our understanding of the nature of and approaches to leadership. Arguably, in the information profession, in which there have always been many women employees and there are now increasing numbers of women in positions where they can or are expected to offer leadership, this issue has important consequences not just within information organizations, but for the profession as a whole.

One way of analysing the research on gender and leadership is to examine the questions that it seeks to answer, the approaches that are adopted, and the factors that might influence any outcomes.

Research questions

There are several questions that can be posed to capture the relationship between gender and leadership. We might start by seeking to explore whether women's leadership styles and approaches are different from those of men. But this is only a start. Typical follow-on questions include:

◆ Are women's' leadership styles likely to be more effective than those of men?
◆ How can women be developed as leaders?
◆ To what extent should leadership development be designed to reinforce or dissipate any differences between the leadership styles of men and women?

Research approaches

Arguably the most important factor that might affect the outcome of the research is the stakeholders who are asked to report. Much research is self-reporting, perhaps using instruments that measure the extent of adoption of one or other of Likert's leadership styles, or whether women are more or less likely than men to adopt a transformational leadership style. All-round evaluation, which encourages both subordinates and more senior managers to evaluate a leader in terms of their leadership style, may reveal differences in perceptions between the various stakeholders. In addition, gender may affect the judgement of leadership style and leader effectiveness (Kabacoff, 2000). Most importantly, all such evaluations and judgements are subjective, and shaped by culture, experience and socialization.

Research influences

Many factors might affect the outcomes of research into the relationship between leadership and gender:

1 *The women themselves*, and aspects such as their attitude towards leadership roles, their self-confidence and their experience. Attitude towards leadership is an important indicator of potential effectiveness. However, the roles that women have been taught to play and the attitudes that they have been encouraged to assume may not help them to identify themselves or be identified by others as potential leaders. Importantly, women's own attitudes may be reinforced by limited encouragement and support in their leadership role. As Cassirer and Reskin (2000) suggest, blocked mobility breeds pessimism and disengagement among workers, whereas indication of opportunity fosters engagement and optimism. Related to attitude is women's self-confidence. An internalized 'second class' attitude may undermine self-confidence, and lead to women accepting less, and satisficing when their leadership skills are not acknowledged. Lack of confidence, in turn, may restrict opportunity and experience.

2 *The corporate environment* might not only affect women's leadership opportunities, but could also impact on outcomes of research into the leadership effectiveness of women. Organizations typically favour stereotypical masculine values, such as being domineering, tough minded and powerful. Examination of women leaders in such environments will be influenced by the embedded notions of what a leader should be.

3 As is discussed further in the next chapter, good leaders *change their style* as they become more experienced and to suit the context in which they find themselves. A key factor is the sector in which the leaders work; different sectors have different dominant values and organizational cultures. It is difficult to understand leadership without reference to organizational culture, and indeed the wider context. In addition, there is some evidence to suggest that as women take on more senior management roles, their leadership style changes, and their identification with the male model of managerial and leadership success

becomes more evident (Grant, 1988; Peters and Kabacoff, 2002). Or is it rather that those women who have a more masculine style are those who succeed and move into more senior positions?

4   Differentiating between men and women as leaders tends to drive towards *stereotypes*. But both men and women are individuals and may adopt a range of different style.

5   *Evaluation of leadership effectiveness*: women's effectiveness as leaders may be measured using different standards from those used to measure effective leadership by men. Men are judged according to values of assertiveness and action-orientation, but women tend to be judged on their ability to create and maintain positive interpersonal relationships (Peters and Kabacoff, 2002).

Having established that there are some difficulties in exploring the relationship between gender and leadership, we now proceed with caution to discuss some of the findings of research in this area. Much deals with the impact of socialization of girls and women. Tannen (1995) focuses on the different communication and relationship-building styles adopted by men and women. She suggests that girls learn to focus on rapport, while boys focus on status. Men are more likely to put others down and to appear knowledgeable and confident. Women are more likely to seek face-saving solutions. Women can appear to lack self-confidence by playing down their certainty and expressing doubt; but women who adopt a 'masculine' linguistic style can be viewed as aggressive.

There is considerable evidence to suggest that women are more people-orientated as leaders, and tend to place greater emphasis on caring and nurturing relationships. Women are more likely to use spoken communication for relationship-building and giving emotional support than men. Women are more collaborative and rational. They score high on leadership scales measuring orientation towards production and results, and are rated highly on people-oriented leadership skills. Men, on the other hand, tend to be more directive and bureaucratic. Men focus more on disseminating information and demonstrating competence. They score highly on business-oriented leadership skills, and on scales assessing an orientation towards strategic planning and organizational vision (Kabacoff, 1998, Oshagbemi and Gill, 2003).

There are some suggestions that with flatter structures and changing environments that require a transformational, rather than a transactional, leadership style, female leadership styles are increasingly relevant to organizations. Such contexts require skills in communication, collaboration, consensus, decision-making, teamwork, networking and developing others – qualities associated with women. There is a growing consensus that the most effective management style may be one that combines masculine and feminine attributes. Described as *androgyny*, this means being decisive and emotionally expressive, independent and tender, aggressive and gentle, assertive and yielding.

Summary and conclusions

The overarching aim of this chapter is to provide you with some concepts, models, tools and perspectives from which to consider your approach to leadership. This chapter should have started you on the road to thinking about yourself and others as leaders. It has deliberately taken a simplistic view of leadership theories, focusing on the notions of traits and styles. Although many of the theories in these areas are long established, they underpin later developments, and re-emerge in the contingency and trans-formational leadership theories that are discussed in the following chapter.

An essential ingredient of any leader is their personality; the first section in this chapter introduces briefly some of the theories on personality, indicating the difference between describing people in terms of a set of traits, or with one label representative of a personality type. The next two sections establish the notions of leadership traits and styles, respectively. Although long-standing, the search for a set of standard traits for leaders continues, and recent work has been conducted on leadership traits for leaders in the information profession. The leadership styles approach is concerned with the identification of appropriate behaviours for leaders. Many of the models focus on the way in which the leader interacts with their followers. Communication is important in the people aspect of leadership; a few useful concepts for considering individual and organizational communication are discussed. The final two sections deal with aspects of leadership that have received considerable attention in recent years. Emotional intelligence, the ability to understand and respond to your own emotions and those of others, is seen as increasingly important as the role of emotions in influencing and motivating people has been considered more explicitly. The relationship between gender and leadership needs consideration partly because of the assumption underlying much earlier leadership literature that leaders are men. An assessment of leadership approaches of men and women suggests that there may be differences, but that gender is only one of many factors that affect leadership style, and in any case the optimum leadership style for the future may involve qualities drawn from both 'masculine' and 'feminine' leadership styles.

Review questions

1 Why are personality trait and type theories useful in thinking about leadership? Give examples.
2 What do you understand by the concept 'leadership trait'? What research has been conducted to discuss the traits of public library leaders?
3 Discuss Likert's systems of leadership, with reference to the relative importance of task centered and people centered behaviour in a leader.
4 Why is communication important to leadership?
5 What is the relationship between emotional intelligence and leadership?
6 Discuss Goleman's four capabilities of emotional intelligence. Give examples.
7 Why is it difficult to research the link between gender and leadership?
8 What does research tell us about the differences between men and women as leaders?

Challenges

1 What is the link between personality and leadership?
2 Are traits a good way of profiling leaders in the information profession?
3 Do leaders need to perform in all facets of the leadership diamond to be effective?
4 Does Likert's model of systems of leadership capture all of the necessary facets of leadership?

5   How can emotional intelligence be measured? What are the dimensions of emotional intelligence?

6   Is emotional intelligence always a good thing?

7   Do men and women lead differently? What are the origins of any differences?

8   If men and women do manage differently, what are the consequences for our notions of an effective leader?

Case study interview with Coral Black, Head of Public Services, Senate House Library, University of London, UK

Biography

Coral is currently Head of Public Services at Senate House Library, the University of London. Previously she was Deputy Head of Learning Services at Edge Hill University, Lancashire (UK), and she has worked as a manager and library and information professional in higher education institutions for over 20 years. Her professional interests focus specifically on customer service and staff management and development. She has written and presented on a range of topics, most recently on leadership development and online approaches to staff training.

1   What have you learnt from psychometric tests about your personality?

I have done a number psychometric tests all of which have provided similar results in terms of my personality and approaches to leadership and my ways of working. The tools that I have used include Myers Briggs, OPQ (Occupational Personality Questionnaire) and Quintax.

The outcomes have not been a surprise but have reinforced my tendencies to be task focused, always looking at actions and outcomes, happy to involve others but on my terms and with a need 'to get the job done'. I have also learnt that I value co-operation and agreement with other people and try to ensure harmony across the team. Through discussion with mentors, colleagues and peers, and my own reflection, I have been able to reflect on my own practice and look specifically at areas that I feel I need to improve. This has included the need to listen more to other people's ideas in terms of change, involve people more in order to achieve our goals and make it fun for myself and others. I have also learnt that I need to look at other ways of doing things, in some ways to be more creative, to take risks and to reflect more on myself, my team and the work we do.

2 In what way do you think your personality affects your approach to leadership?

I think my personality means that I am continually balancing the need to move things forward against the impact this will have on the team and how staff will manage the changes that need to take place. This takes a great deal of effort as I try to ensure people are engaged, motivated and happy with the changes that are taking place. I think on the whole this has worked well and I don't feel that service delivery and change has been compromised in terms of timescales.

3 How do you balance the conflict between getting the task done and managing the people issues?

'Getting the job done' is always a priority for me but I am ever conscious of the need to bring the team with me in order to achieve this. My approach is to be very open with staff, be clear about expectations both in terms of what they can expect from me but also what I expect from them. In doing this I always give people the opportunity to discuss concerns with what we are trying to achieve. Over the years I have developed a more consultative approach in developing strategy, setting objectives and future priorities. This has ensured that staff at all levels are fully engaged and all moving in the same direction. Another area I have focused on relates to getting the best from the team and looking at strengths rather than weaknesses in terms of knowledge and skills. This has resulted in staff working on projects that match their skills and interests and results in greater commitment.

4 How would you describe your leadership style?

I adopt a consultative approach, engaging staff at all levels of the team in discussion and future planning. I pay attention to opinions and feelings of other, but I am able to keep a clear sense of priorities and what needs to 'get done'. I feel that I am very fair but firm in terms of how I deal with people and staff know what I expect from them.

5 Do you think that managers should be expected to exercise emotional intelligence?

Yes, I think it is so important to understand how as a manager your behaviour can impact on others and how this can impact both positively and negatively in staff performance. It is also important to understand that all staff are different in terms of what motivates them, how they want to be treated and how to get the best out of them in terms of the working environment. By exercising EI a manager can deal with difficult situations in a positive way that reduces hostility, develops a more collaborative approach to team working and enhances team spirit.

6 Do you think that men and women lead differently? If so, in what ways?

Mmm, I'm not really sure about this one. I don't necessarily feel that women lead in one way and men another. I do feel that in my experience women tend to think more about the people they are working with and how they can get the best out of them. They are often more consultative in their approach while men can be more autocratic in their leadership.

References and additional reading

Appelbaum, S. H., Audet, L. and Miller, J. C. (2003) Gender and Leadership? Leadership and gender? A journey through the landscape of theories, *Leadership & Organization Development Journal*, **24** (1), 43–51.

Barling, J., Slater, F. and Kelloway, E. K. (2000) Transformational Leadership and Emotional Intelligence: an exploratory study, *Leadership & Organization Development Journal*, **21** (3), 157–61.

Cassirer, N. and Reskin, B. (2000) High Hopes: organizational position, employment experiences, and women's and men's promotion aspirations, *Work and Occupations*, **27** (4), 438–63.

Cole, G. A. (2004) *Management Theory and Practice*, 6th edn, London, Thomson.

Covey, S. R. (1992) *Principled Centred Leadership*, New York, Simon and Schuster.

Debowski, S. (2006) *Knowledge Management*, Milton, Queensland, Australia, Wiley (chapter 3 – the knowledge leader).

Department of Health (2002) *NHS Leadership Qualities Framework*, London, Modernisation Agency, The NHS Leadership Centre.

Dewey, B. I. (1998) Public Services Librarians in the Academic Community: the imperative for leadership. In Mech, T. F. and McCabe, G. B. (eds), *Leadership and Academic Librarians*, Westport, CT, Greenwood Press, 85–107.

Dulewicz. V. and Higgs, M. (2000) Emotional Intelligence – a review and evaluation study, *Journal of Managerial Psychology*, **15** (4), 341–68.

Gibb, J. R. (1961) *Defensive Communication*, **11**, 41–9.

Goleman, D. (2000) Leadership That Gets Results, *Harvard Business Review*, **78** (2), 78–90.

Grant, J. (1988) Women as Managers: what they can offer to organizations, *Organizational Dynamics*, **16** (3), 56–63.

Huczynski, A (2004) *Influencing Within Organizations*, London, Routledge.

Huczynski, A. A. and Buchanan, D. A. (2007) Organizational Behaviour, 6th edn, Harlow, FT Prentice Hall.

Humphrey, R. H. (2002) The Many Faces of Emotional Leadership, *Leadership Quarterly*, **13** (5), 493–504.

Kabacoff, R. I. (1998) *Gender Differences in Organisational Leadership: a large sample study*, Portland, ME, Management Research Group.

Kabacoff, R. I. (2000) Gender and Leadership in the Corporate Boardroom. Paper presented to the 108th Annual Convention of the American Psychological Association, Washington, DC.

Kernbach, S. and Schutte, N. S. (2005) The Impact of Service Provider Emotional Intelligence on Customer Satisfaction, *Journal of Services Marketing*, **19** (7), 438–44.

Kerr, R., Garvi, J., Heaton, N. and Boyle, E. (2006) Emotional Intelligence and Leadership Effectiveness. *Leadership and Organization Development Journal*, **27** (4), 265–79.

Kolb, J. (1999) The Effect of Gender Role on Attitude Toward Leadership, and Self-confidence on Leader Emergence: implications for leadership development, *Human Resource Development Quarterly*, **10** (4), 305–20.

Likert, R. (1961) *New Patterns of Management*, New York, McGraw-Hill.

Mattis, M. C. (2001) Advancing Women in Business Organizations: key leadership roles and behaviors of senior leaders and middle managers, *Journal of Management Development*, **20** (4), 371–88.

Mayer, J. D., Caruso, D. R. and Salovey, P. (2000) Emotional Intelligence as Zeitgeist, as Personality, and as a Mental Ability. In Bar-On, R. and Parker, J. D. A. (eds), *The Handbook of Emotional Intelligence: theory, development, assessment, and application at home school and in the workplace*, New York, Jossey-Bass/Wiley.

Mead, G. H. (1934) *Mind, Self and Society*, Chicago, University of Chicago Press.

Mullins, J. and Linehan, M. (2006) Desired Qualities of Public Library Leaders, *Leadership and Organization Development Journal*, **27** (2), 133–43.

Mullins, L. J. (2005) *Management and Organizational Behaviour*, 7th edn, Harlow, FT Prentice Hall.

Noble, C. and Moore, S. (2006) Advancing Women and Leadership in this Post Feminist, Post EEO Era, *Women in Management Review*, **21** (7), 598–603.

Oshagbemi, T. and Gill, R. (2003) Gender Different and Similarities in the Leadership Styles and Behavior of UK Managers, *Women in Management Review*, **18** (6), 288–98.

Peters, H. and Kabacoff, R. I. (2002) *Leadership and Gender: a new look at the glass ceiling*, MRG Research Report, Portland, ME, Management Research Group.

Regan, H. B. and Brooks, G. H. (1995) *Out of Women's Experience: creating relational leadership*, Thousand Oaks, CA, Corwin Press.

Rosengeld, P., Giacalone, R. A. and Riordan, C. A. (2001) *Impression Management: building and enhancing reputations at work*, London, Thomson Learning.

Stewart, R. (1963) *The Reality of Management*, London, Pan/Heinemann.

Tannen, D. (1995) The Power of Talk: who gets heard and why, *Harvard Business Review*, **73** (5), 138–48.

Wicks, D. and Bradshaw, P. (1999) Gendered Organizational Cultures in Canadian Work Organizations: implications for creating an equitable workplace, *Management Decision*, **37** (4), 372–80.

3

Leadership in context

Learning objectives

After reading this chapter you should be able to:

- ☑ appreciate the impact of context on effective leadership behaviours
- ☑ understand the difference between transformational and transactional leadership
- ☑ reflect on leadership in practice and the leadership experience.

Introduction

From a theoretical perspective this chapter continues the exploration of different models of leadership. The previous chapter examined the trait and style theories of leadership and encouraged you to engage with how they can be used to reflect on your understanding of what leadership is, and how leaders behave. This chapter moves on to consider three more recent groups of theories: contingency theories, transformational leadership theories and theories that consider leadership in practice and the leadership experience. Contingency theories suggest that the most effective leadership style depends on, or is contingent on the context; they identify key aspects of the context and classify leadership styles and behaviours in relation to these different types of context. Transformational leadership theories seek to explore the leadership behaviours necessary to engage and motivate followers. Leadership theories that focus on leadership in practice and the leadership experience explore the leadership process and in particular seek to contribute to leadership development.

Context and contingency theories of leadership

The Michigan and Ohio leadership theories discussed in Chapter 2 suggest that the 'high consideration, high structure' approach is the 'one best way'. Although managing people and a task might intuitively seem to be essential aspects of leadership behaviour in any context, behaviour that is expected of, and respected in, staff and their leaders is different in different sectors, depending on the objectives of the organization. For example, the head of a national library, such as the British Library, is expected to develop and evolve a vision for the role of the library that they lead in a national and international marketplace, and this involves leadership on national and international platforms. Vision, careful management of power and politics, and reputation management are required, and these are key qualities for leaders. On the other hand, the leader of an electronic resources team in a public library, although also needing to manage the politics and power issues around resources and to develop a credible vision for developing their service, is required to focus on leading their team to ensure reliable and effective service delivery. There is a much greater focus on developing the team in this example.

Many members of information services teams are professionals. Mintzberg (1998) suggests that as knowledge work grows in importance managers will be increasingly managing other professionals so the leader will not have all of the power. He discusses the 'covert leadership' exercised by an orchestral conductor as a model for leadership in knowledge-intensive organizations. When exercising covert leadership leaders guide without seeming to, and operate with a sense of nuances, constraints and limitations. The emphasis is on inspiring, rather than empowering, because followers are already empowered by their own knowledge and skills.

The most appropriate style may also depend on the core values and object-ives of an organization. In two somewhat opposing contributions, Politis

(2001) discusses the best leadership style to achieve knowledge acquisition within an organization and suggests that participative decision-making processes are the way forward, while Van Wart (2003) reflects on the lack of sophistication in public sector leadership theory because of the impact of bureaucracy, tensions between political and administrative roles, and public sector accountability.

Contingency theories offer some insights into the key contextual factors that might influence optimum leadership behaviour. Below we consider five key theories, indicating the common ground between them and the differences in their perspectives. Unfortunately there is no neat and tidy package of theory which can be picked up and applied in practice, but together these theories help in thinking about what it means to say that context affects what is deemed to be effective leadership behaviour.

Adair's action-centred leadership

Adair's (1979) model of action-centred leadership was not explicitly recognized as a contingency approach, in the sense that its focus is not on the different leadership styles for different situations, but rather on what leaders actually do. Nevertheless from this perspective Adair identified some of the key functions that leaders fulfil, and thereby some of the potential variables that may change between leadership situations. Adair's model suggests that the effectiveness of the leader depends on their fulfilment of task functions, team functions and individual functions:

◆ *task functions* – achieving the objectives of the work group, defining group tasks, planning the work, allocation of resources and organization of duties and responsibilities
◆ *team functions* – maintaining morale and building team spirit, the cohesiveness of the group as a working unit, setting standards and maintaining the discipline, systems of communication within the group, training the group and appointing sub-leaders
◆ *individual functions* – meeting the needs of the individual members of the group, attending to personal problems, giving praise and status,

reconciling conflicts between group needs and needs of the individual, and training the individual.

One of the important facets of Adair's theory is the separate identification of the team and the individual, which in many other models is consolidated into a general concern for people or relationships. Team leadership and the roles of leaders in teams are discussed in more detail in Chapter 5.

The Tannenbaum–Schmidt continuum of leadership

Tannenbaum and Schmidt (1958) laid the foundations for the contingency school of leadership by making the basic proposition that different leadership styles are appropriate in different contexts. They also suggested there is a continuum of leadership styles, with democratic and autocratic at the two extremes, as shown in Figure 3.1. They argued that the most appropriate point on their leadership continuum depended on the context, and specifically on three sets of forces:

◆ *forces in the manager* – personality, background, knowledge, values, preference, beliefs about employee participation, confidence in subordinates, feelings of security, and leadership inclinations
◆ *forces in the subordinates* – need for independence, tolerance of ambiguity, knowledge of and interest in the problem, expectations of involvement, identification with organizational goals
◆ *forces in the situation* – organizational norms, size and location of work groups, effectiveness of team working, nature of the problem, type of organization, and time pressures.

Boss-centred leadership				**Subordinate-centred leadership**		
Manager makes decision and announces it	Manager 'sells' decision	Manager presents ideas and invites questions	Manager presents tentative decision subject to change	Manager presents problem, gets suggestions, makes decision	Manager defines limits, asks group to make decision	Manager permits subordinates to function within limits defined by superior

Figure 3.1 Leadership behaviours in the Tannenbaum and Schmidt continuum of leadership

Although the term 'forces' might not seem particularly appropriate, within their three categories Tannenbaum and Schmidt identify a wide range of potential factors that might influence leadership behaviour. Their lists are, in fact, more wide ranging than those explicitly discussed by some later authors. For example, organizational norms, location of working groups, values and preference are typically overlooked by later theories. Tannenbaum and Schmidt argue that successful leaders are aware of these forces and are able to behave appropriately; they are both perceptive and flexible.

Fiedler's contingency theory of leadership

Fiedler's (1967) contribution to contingency theory was to establish that leadership effectiveness was not only influenced by leadership orientation but also by:

◆ *task structure* – the extent to which the task in hand is structured and defined for the group
◆ *position power* – the power of the leader and extent to which they can exercise authority to influence
◆ *leader–member relations* – the nature of the relationship between the leader and followers.

On the basis of these factors, Fiedler identified eight combinations of group-task situations that relate to leadership style. There are three typical sets of conditions under which a leader may operate:

Condition 1

◆ The task is highly structured.
◆ The leader's position power is high.
◆ Subordinates feel that their relationships with the boss are good.

Under Condition 1, relationships can to some extent be taken for granted, and therefore task-oriented leaders get good results.

Condition 2

◆ The task is unstructured.

◆ The leader's position power is low.

◆ Subordinates feel that their relationships with the boss are moderately good.

Relationship-orientated leaders perform best in such circumstances because effort directed towards relationship maintenance is repaid.

Condition 3

◆ The task is unstructured.

◆ The leader's position power is low.

◆ Subordinates feel that their relationships with the boss are poor.

These are difficult conditions, in which task-orientated leaders get better results, because the task-oriented leader focuses on the task and tries to structure and control the situation, and does not allow the agenda to be sidetracked into over-focus on repairing damaged and sometimes irreparable relationships.

Fiedler's theory offers another perspective on the factors that might influence leadership effectiveness. He argued that leadership effectiveness may be improved by changing the leadership situation. However, these conditions assume 'one point in time', and therefore perhaps do not fully explore the extent to which the actions that leaders might take (whether they be relationship or task oriented) over a period of time might impact on the level of task structure, their position power, power from other sources (e.g. social power) and relationship building. Fiedler proposes that leaders cannot change their style to fit a context, but that they should choose a context to fit their style. In practice this is often easier said than done; in new leadership roles it can be difficult to predict factors such as position power, level of task structure and relationships. In addition, when compared with some of the other leadership theories, Fiedler might be viewed as offering only a limited range of factors to be taken into account in determining leadership behaviour.

REFLECTION As a follower have you ever experienced a new manager tackle a situation under Fiedler's Condition 3? Discuss the manager's behaviour in this context and evaluate whether they offered effective leadership.

Vroom and Yetton's contingency model of leadership

Vroom and Yetton (1973) suggest decision rules to help the manager discover the most appropriate decision style in a given situation. Together these rules affect the:

◆ *decision quality* – the effect that the decision has on group performance
◆ *decision acceptance* – the motivation and commitment of group members in implementing the decision.

They suggest using decision tree charts to indicate which decision style should be adopted. Perhaps one of the most interesting aspects of one of their later pieces of work is the list of contingency factors that they develop. They suggest and use the following contingency variables:

◆ quality requirement
◆ commitment requirement
◆ leader information
◆ problem structure
◆ commitment probability
◆ goal congruence
◆ subordinate conflict
◆ subordinate information
◆ time constraint
◆ geographical dispersion
◆ motivation time
◆ motivation development.

Hersey and Blanchard situational leadership theory

Situational leadership theory describes leader behaviour in terms of two dimensions:

- *task behaviour* – the amount of direction a leader gives to subordinates
- *supportive behaviour* – the amount of social back-up a leader gives to subordinates.

Today we might baulk at the use of the word subordinates and prefer to use the term follower. Nevertheless, interestingly, the focus remains on task and relationships as the two key aspects of leader behaviour. On this basis, Hersey and Blanchard (1988) propose four different leadership styles:

- *telling* – high amounts of task behaviour, telling followers what to do, when to do it and how to do it, but with little relationship behaviour; the leader provides specific instructions and supervises performance
- *selling* – high amounts of task behaviour and relationship behaviour; the leader explains decisions and provides opportunities for clarification
- *participating* – lots of relationship behaviour and support, but little direction or task behaviour; the leader shares ideas and facilitates follower's decision making
- *delegating* – not much task or relationship behaviour; the leader turns over responsibility for decisions and their implementation to followers.

As a set of styles this is interesting and useful in articulating the control that the leader chooses to allow followers to exert. It does, however, assume that the leader always has control, and that followers are compliant with the leader's wishes, and begs many questions about whether leaders should adopt different approaches in different contexts, and the factors that determine when each style is appropriate. Hersey and Blanchard offer the concept of *follower readiness* as an important factor in determining the most appropriate leadership style. Follower readiness is captured on a follower readiness continuum based on the follower's ability, willingness and level of confidence, which has the following states:

- able and willing or confident
- able but unwilling or insecure
- unable but willing or confident
- unable and unwilling or insecure.

Hersey and Blanchard then superimpose the readiness continuum on the possible leadership styles, suggesting that unable and unwilling or insecure followers need telling, whereas able and willing or confident followers flourish under delegation. This match between leadership style and follower characteristics is important and interesting, but in order to operationalize this approach fully the leader needs to understand and respond to the factors that make followers unable and unwilling or insecure, or indeed able and willing or confident. In addition a leader is often faced with a team whose members have different levels of ability, experience and confidence. The real challenge is then to create a consistent team leadership approach that builds trust and a sense of where the team is going, while also appropriately accommodating the leadership needs of individuals. For all that this is difficult if leadership is exercised from a position of supervisor or manager, it is much more challenging to respond to followers' leadership needs in a matrix, project or other group situation in which it may not even be clear who the followers should be, let alone who is inclined to follow. Chapter 5 explores the issues of followership further.

Recent research that examined the application of Hersey and Blanchard's situational leadership theory in organizations in Taiwan highlights specifically the continuing need to investigate the usefulness and relevance of such theories in non-Western contexts, and also raises a number of issues about the relationships between the variables in this model. Chen and Silverstone (2005) found that a match between leadership style and subordinate readiness did not result in a higher level of subordinate job satisfaction and performance, and lower levels of job stress and intention to leave. However, they found that the higher the leadership score, the more effective is the leader's influence.

REFLECTION Think of a situation in which you have wanted to influence people. To what extent have you accommodated your understanding of the characteristics of the followers? Which characteristics have you taken into account?

Goleman's leadership styles

On the basis of a significant and relatively recent research project, Goleman (2000) identified six leadership styles that impact on 'working atmosphere' and 'financial performance'. These styles are summarized in Table 3.1, which shows their labels, what the style asks in practice, the competencies required of the leader, and when it is appropriate to use the style. Goleman suggests that a good leader has a portfolio of leadership styles and uses them as appropriate, knowing when to switch styles as the situation commands. This position has moved a long way from the earlier trait and style theories where personality is seen as a key determinant of leadership style. This position may represent an evolution of what is expected and required of a leader as organizational climates have become more volatile and all employees are expected to be adaptable.

Table 3.1 Goleman's six leadership styles (based on Goleman, 2000)

Style	In practice	In a phrase	Competencies	When to use
Coercive	Demands compliance	'Do what I tell you'	Drive to achieve, initiative, self-control	In a crisis, or with problem employees
Authoritative	Mobilizes people towards a vision	'Come with me'	Self-confidence, empathy, change catalyst	When new vision and clear direction is needed
Affiliative	Creates harmony and emotional bonds	'People come first'	Empathy, relationships, communication	To heal rifts and wounds, to motivate people under stress
Democratic	Forges consensus through participation	'What do you think?'	Collaboration, teambuilding	To build consensus and buy-in, to get contributions
Pacesetting	Sets high performance standards	'Do as I do, now'	Initiative, drive to achieve	To get fast results from a motivated and competent team
Coaching	Develops people for the future	'Try this'	Empathy, self-awareness	To improve performance, to develop long-term strengths

Goleman suggests that coercion and pacesetting need to be used with caution as they can damage the 'working atmosphere' by reducing flexibility and employee commitment. The other four styles always have a positive impact on climate and performance when exercised appropriately. In order to develop such a portfolio of skills, individuals need to reflect and learn from a range of different leadership experiences in different contexts. The development of leadership competencies under this model may be a relatively lengthy process, and it might be argued that Goleman's portfolio idea is an aspiration rather than a reality for many managers and others in leadership positions merely because they do not always have the opportunity to change their experience and context sufficiently to acquire competence in exercising a full set of leadership styles.

REFLECTION Which of Goleman's leadership styles might be appropriate in the following situation?

You have just been appointed as university librarian. The library is held in very low regard across the university, and has been under funded for many years, which has stifled innovation and development. Staff are unaccustomed to change, are demoralized by a recent redundancy programme, and cannot see how any further changes could possibly be in their own best interest.

Justify your suggestion.

Leadership contingent on business stage

Some authors have explored one aspect of the leadership situation further, the stage of development of a business. They suggest that different style of leadership may be appropriate at different stages in the development of an organization. For example, Clark and Pratt (1985) identify the following styles of managerial leadership:

◆ *champion* – appropriate for a new ventures when the leader must be able to drive a small team to win orders, provide a wide range of management skills, and have the energy and commitment to address a range of different matters
◆ *tank commander* – appropriate as the business enters a growth stage, when the manager needs to develop a strong, supportive team and be able to make significant inroads into the market
◆ *housekeeper* – appropriate in the mature stage of the business, when the business is operating in a competitive market; key here are efficient and economic management of the businesses, involving planning, cost control and sound personnel policies
◆ *lemon-squeezer* – appropriate should a business go into decline; in order to try to revitalize the business, the lemon squeezer needs to be tough

and innovative in cutting costs, improving productivity and managing staffing levels.

Clark and Pratt suggest that few leaders are sufficiently adaptable to be able to adopt all of these roles.

Rodrigues (1987, 1993) also agreed that different types of leaders are needed at different stages of the development of a company, and suggested three types of leader:

◆ *the innovator*, to support the problem solving stage of business development, where identifying and selling new ideas is key
◆ *the implementer*, to support the implementation stage of development, with a focus on accomplishing things through people, a systematic approach and confidence in decision making
◆ *the pacifier*, to support the stable stage, where it is important to decentralize decision making, to pacify important individuals, and to manage social interaction and working relationships.

Criticisms of contingency theories

Contingency theories of leadership are useful because they encourage reflection on the context of leadership, including the follower, the task and the leader's power relationships. In general they reject the notion that there is one leadership style that will always produce the best outcomes. On the other hand, there are a number of criticisms of contingency theories, some of which are discussed below.

1 There is a strong argument in support of the value of democratic or participative leadership. Participative leadership or management improves organizational effectiveness because it gathers ideas from people who have knowledge and experience; people who are involved in making decisions are more likely to be committed to those decisions and their consequences; in addition, participation reflects democratic, social and political values. Indeed, some practitioners use the older models on style discussed in Chapter 2, and suggest that, for example, Likert's systems of leadership can be used as a basis for the different

styles to match different circumstances. These models often also introduce different leadership styles, and different definitions of contexts.

2   The variables identified in the contingency theories vary between theories, and are vague and loosely defined. Further there are a number of aspects of the context that are not explicitly addressed by these theories such as organization culture, change processes, personality, stress, motivation, working conditions, job design, organizational structures and technology. Indeed, there are often organizational norms concerning what is acceptable leadership style.

3   Whether leaders can adapt their style to fit the context is debatable, because these theories seem to leave the issue of personality to one side. For example, the leader, who feels comfortable coaching and developing people, may be very uncomfortable and ineffective if the situation demands that they be coercive.

4   Managers who change their style (and thereby the way in which they interact with people) may be viewed as inconsistent and unpredictable. This may not be the best basis for building a good working atmosphere, trust and strong working relationships.

These criticisms do not invalidate contingency theories, but they do indicate the complexities of the relationship between leadership style and organizational context. Leaders need to change and be adaptable in different roles and contexts. Contingency theories offer some tools to support analysis of situations, but they are not the complete solution.

REFLECTION Describe the 'acceptable' leadership style in an organization known to you.

The context for the information profession and its implications for leadership

The theories that have been reviewed so far in this chapter are general theories from the literature of management and organizational behaviour. There is considerable scope for examining these theories in the context of the information profession. Undoubtedly, in this context there are people and tasks, and different approaches to leadership, so these theories are a useful starting point. The most interesting question is: What are the characteristics of the context of leadership in the information profession that might influence the choice of leadership style?

Transformational and transactional leadership

New leadership, a leadership theory that originated with the work of Burns (1978), proposed a distinction between transformational and transactional leaders. The new or transformational leader is an inspirational visionary who is concerned to build a shared sense of purpose and mission, and to create a culture in which everyone is aligned with the organization's goals and is skilled and empowered to achieve them. Such transformational leaders are charismatic individuals who inspire and motivate others to perform beyond their contract. The transformational leader treats relationships with followers in terms of motivation and commitment, influencing and inspiring followers to give more than compliance towards improvement of organizational performance: they encourage commitment, initiative, flexibility and high performance. This is in contrast to transactional leaders who enact their relationships with followers in terms of an exchange, giving the followers what they want in return for what the leader desires, on the basis of prescribed tasks to pursue established goals.

REFLECTION Here are three questions that might challenge long-standing assumptions:

1 Why do we bind journals?
2 Why do we buy newspapers?
3 What use could we make of CCTV?

What would be the reaction in your organization to a junior member of staff who posed one or more such questions?

Some writers have aligned transformational leadership with leadership and transactional leadership with management (e.g. Bartram and Brown, 2006).

Castiglione (2006) suggests that the transactional library administrator is assignment and task-oriented, and expects employee compliance. The transformational library administrator, on the other hand, inspires, motivates and facilitates strategic renewal by empowering staff to question old assumptions; they encourage staff to construct a compelling vision of future possibilities for themselves and their stakeholders.

Bass and Avolio (1990, 1994) further articulate the concept of transformational leadership by suggesting that transformational leaders use the four Is:

◆ *intellectual stimulation* – encouraging others to see what they are doing from new perspectives and thereby promoting innovation and creativity from followers
◆ *idealized influence* – through articulating and interpreting the mission or vision of the organization, gaining the respect and admiration of others
◆ *individualized consideration* – with a focus on developing others to higher levels of ability
◆ *inspirational motivation* – seeking to motivate others to place organizational interests above and before those of their own self-interest, and to give meaning and challenge to the work of followers.

The Transformational Leadership Questionnaire (Alimo-Metcalfe and Alban-Metcalfe, 2002, 2003) approaches transformational leadership from the standpoint of a collection of 14 leadership behaviours, which they group into three categories as shown in Figure 3.2. They found evidence to suggest that these behaviours can increase job satisfaction and motivation and reduce stress. Women were perceived as more transformational than men on most of these behaviours, and were rated as better than men at being decisive, focusing effort, mentoring, managing change, inspiring others and being open to ideas.

The focus on the identification of transformational, visionary and charismatic new leaders might appear to be at odds with the concept of informal leadership at all levels and associated with a variety of roles in an organization. But, Alimo-Metcalfe and Alban-Metcalfe (2002) propose a twin track approach in which there is a focus both on transformational leaders and on

Leading and developing others by:
- showing genuine concern
- empowering
- being accessible
- encouraging change

Personal qualities:
- being transparent
- acting with integrity
- being decisive
- inspiring others
- resolving complex problems

Leading the organization by:
- networking and achieving
- focusing team effort
- building shared vision
- supporting a developmental culture
- facilitating change sensitively.

Figure 3.2 Transformational Leadership Questionnaire behaviours

leadership capacity throughout the organization. The concept of dispersed leadership derives from the observation that leadership is best exercised by those who have the interest, knowledge, skills and motivation to perform specific leadership functions and roles. This concept has resonances with team role theory and self-directed teams, discussed further in Chapter 5. This twin track approach is embedded in the model created by Bennis and Nanus (1985) of *'twenty-first century' leadership* as summarized in Table 3.2. The development of leadership capacity throughout the organization makes particular demands on senior leaders, and this has led to the concept of a super leader. A *super leader* develops leadership capacity in others, empowering them, reducing their dependence on formal leaders and stimulating their motivation, commitment and creativity.

Transformational leadership offers some useful perspectives on the leadership behaviours that might inspire and motivate others. It has been developed alongside models of dispersed leadership, which propose the development of leadership capacity throughout the organization.

Table 3.2 The Bennis-Nanus model of 21st-century leadership (Bennis and Nanus, 1985)

From	To
Few top leaders	Leaders at every level, few managers
Leading by goal-setting	Leading by vision, new directions
Downsizing, benchmarking, quality	Create distinctive competencies
Reactive, adaptive to change	Creative, anticipative future change
Design hierarchical organizations	Design flat, collegial organizations
Direct and supervise	Empower, inspire, facilitate
Information held by few decision makers	Information shared with many
Leader as boss, controlling	Leader as coach, creating learning organization
Leader as stabilizer, balancing conflicts	Leader as change agent, balancing risks
Leader develops good managers	Leader develops future leaders

REFLECTION If a super leader develops others so that they rely less on formal leaders, what are the potential consequences for the super leader, and how might they respond creatively?

The literature on the use of transformational management in the information profession is woefully thin. Castiglione (2006) confirms this and suggests that more work is needed in this field in the USA, and there is little reason to suppose that practice elsewhere in the world is much more advanced.

Leadership practice and experience

In recent years there has been increasing concern that the leadership literature that focuses on traits, styles and contexts is not as helpful as it might be in informing individuals and organizations about leadership experience and practice. Extant literature tends, with the exception of the literature on emotional intelligence, to focus on cognitive elements, and to make statements about what a leader is and how they should behave, with very limited reference to how a leader achieves such behaviours. As such they have limited relevance to leadership development. In particular, they offer no real insights into the experience of leadership, including the internal angst, emotions, self doubt, thoughts and feelings associated with being a leader, and which some would argue are central to a leader's developmental journey.

From a practical perspective the key questions to which organizations seek answers are:

◆ What determines who becomes a leader, and how do people emerge as potential leaders?
◆ What determines leadership effectiveness and performance?
◆ How can leadership effectiveness be measured? This involves the development of appropriate instruments for the measurement of leadership effectiveness and performance.

Both of the topics in this section, leadership competencies and leadership experiences, are revisited in Chapter 7 when we discuss leadership development. This section provides context for that discussion, and also completes our exploration of some of the key theoretical frameworks that inform leadership theory and practice.

Leadership practice and leadership competencies

Coming from an applied research and consultancy perspective, Bartram and the SHL Group have sought to develop tools that assist organizations and individuals in those organizations to understand leadership in practice. Key to their work is the definition of leadership competencies, which they define as sets of behaviours that are instrumental in the delivery of desired results or outcomes (Bartram, Robertson and Callinan, 2002). On this basis they define a competency model, the SHL Universal Competency Framework (Bartram, 2005), which is a hierarchical framework with eight broad competency factors (the Great Eight) at the top, 20 more specific competency dimensions below that, and 112 detailed competency components at the bottom. Table 3.3 organizes competency dimensions in terms of their four leadership functions: developing the vision, sharing the goals, gaining support and delivering success. As these competencies are broad collections of behaviours they are neither purely transactional nor purely transformational, and one competency may embrace competency components in either group. Nevertheless, as shown in Table 3.3, the model allows competencies to be broadly grouped into transactional focus and transformational focus.

Table 3.3 The competencies in the SHL Universal Competency Framework

		Competencies	
		Transactional focus	**Transformational focus**
1	Developing the vision: the strategy domain	Analysing Learning and researching Entrepreneurial and commercial thinking	Creating and innovating Formulating strategies and concepts Adapting and responding to change
2	Sharing the goals: the communication domain	Presenting and communicating information Writing and reporting	Relating and networking Persuading and influencing
3	Gaining support: the people domain	Working with people Adhering to principles and values	Leading and supervising
4	Delivering success: the operational domain	Planning and organizing Delivering results Coping with pressure and setbacks	Deciding and initiating action

A number of different points of interest emerge from this work (Bartram and Brown, 2006):

1   It is useful to distinguish between leadership potential or emergence, and leadership performance, and different phases within the life span of a leadership role.

2   Cognitive ability (particularly numerical reasoning) was found to be strongly related to the emergence of the leader. Managers who get promoted into leadership positions are on average more intelligent and more motivated, particularly by achievement, power and commercial outlook, than those in the general management 'pool'.

3   There are differences in the ratings of leadership effectiveness depending on whether the rating is performed by subordinates, line managers or peers. This difference is important because it means that leaders often find it difficult to adopt a leadership style that is regarded as effective by all stakeholders; the compromises that this involves are likely to generate dilemmas and tensions in the leader.

4   There are significant links between the personality of the leader and their effectiveness as seen by other people, although there are some

variations in assessment between categories of rater. Ratings by subordinates, for example, displayed strong links between personality, motivation and performance in the people, communication and operational domains, domains that are easily observable by this category of rater. They see qualities such as diplomacy, consideration and integrity to be desirable in a leader. Peer ratings provided most observations towards the communications domain, emphasizing that extraverted individuals are more likely to obtain effectiveness in 'sharing the goals', since they are likely to invest time with people. Line managers focus on the operational domain, viewing successful leaders as reserved and conscientious.

5   There may be a difference between behaviours that advance a manager's career along the leadership pipeline and behaviours that make for effective organizations. In leadership development it is important to focus on the leader in context, and to consider the impact of specific leadership competencies and behaviours on the organization.

More specific to the information and knowledge context, Allredge and Nilan (2000) report work on knowledge leadership competencies in 3M, an organization which aims to reflect knowledge management principles in its culture and working context. The company identified 12 leadership competencies, which are grouped into three categories:

◆ *fundamental principles* – ethics, integrity, intellectual rigour, and moral judgement
◆ *essential processes* – customer orientation, people management and performance
◆ *visionary leadership* – the development of a global outlook, strategic perspective, encouraging innovation, building relationships, and encouraging flexibility and adaptability.

They use these leadership competencies to assess the leadership capabilities of people, develop potential leaders and select and place leaders in key positions.

In conclusion, an examination of leadership in practice moves us forward from notions of what a leader should be like to the practical issues of promoting and cultivating leadership in organizations. This encourages reflection on the difference between leadership emergence and leadership effectiveness, and in particular highlights the very real difficulties associated with developing a shared notion of what constitutes an effective leader that accommodates the perspective of different stakeholders. The concept of leadership competencies is a useful tool along the journey to measuring effectiveness, and other factors such as the link between leader behaviours and personality and motivation, but there is more work to do in the articulation of sets of leadership competencies.

Leadership experiences and authentic leadership

There is a growing body of research that argues that the extant leadership literature is unhelpful to practising leaders because it does not reflect sufficiently on the experience of being a leader. There is no discussion of the internal angst, emotions, questioning, self-doubt, or thoughts and feelings associated with the different experiences of being a leader, and no exploration of the subjective processes that constitute a leader's developmental journey. Research on the leadership experience centres on the concept of authentic leadership. Authentic leadership is achieved through self-awareness, self-acceptance, authentic actions and relationships, while recognizing one's own vulnerabilities (Luthans and Avolio, 2003). Authentic leadership is concerned with owning one's own experiences, including thoughts, emotions, needs, wants and preferences; acting in accordance with one's true self; expressing what you think and feel, and behaving accordingly. Theorists in this area suggest that authentic leaders are highly self-aware; have clearly defined and therefore strongly articulated values; what they say is consistent with what they believe; and they have ongoing drive and motivation towards natural goals and the ability to harness followership.

The Authentic Leadership Framework (Gardner et al., 2005) has three key elements: trigger events, values and emotions:

1 *Trigger events* – Life trigger events trigger personal growth and development and serve as a catalyst for heightened levels of leader self-awareness. They may relate to underlying facts such as a general

motivation to succeed, or to learn, or they may have a more direct link with leadership experience, but they all affect a leadership approach. Such experiences, which may often be negative events or crises, enable the fine tuning of qualities such as determination, drive, commitment, independence and toughness, and may trigger deep changes in an individual's self-identity.

2   *Values* – Authentic leaders are guided by a set of values that are oriented towards what is 'right' and 'fair' for all stakeholders, including trustworthiness, credibility and moral worth. These values are part of their self-identity and authentic leaders hold these values to be true not because these values are socially or politically appropriate, but because they have experienced them to be true; this makes such leaders 'originals not copies'. Values are highly personalized through lived experiences, experienced emotions and active processes of reflection on those experience and emotions. Values can be categorized into those relating to '*self enhancement*': achievement, pursuit of personal success, power, dominance over others, personal gratification and hedonism; and to '*self transcendence*': benevolence, concern for immediate others, and universalism concerned with the welfare of all people. Turner and Marvin (2006) suggest that leaders fluctuate between the two, returning to the self-enhancement arena to re-charge themselves during their leadership journeys.

3   *Emotions* – Goleman (see Chapter 2) and more recent writers (Turnbull James and Arroba, 2005) argue that it is increasingly important for leaders to understand and use emotion within their organizations. Traditional leadership literature is inclined to view emotions as agents that impair or distort an individual's perceptual or cognitive faculties. Leaders, while emotional in their abilities to inspire, motivate and lead, do not experience emotions, and, in particular, are free from negative emotions. Some would argue that leaders have the emotional capacity to tolerate uncertainty, frustration and pain without getting too anxious themselves; communicating confidence, counteracting distractions such as scapegoating and projections of negative emotions onto other groups while developing collective self-confidence. On the other hand, leaders need confidence in their capacity to contribute by relying on their

personal authority. In order to lead they must bring a lot of themselves and their identity into the workplace: their ideas, feelings, values, excitement, enthusiasms and inner authority guide their behaviour, decisions and choices; this makes them vulnerable. In the search for rational, controlled and emotionless leaders emotions and emotionality becomes pushed underground and hidden beneath the surface. Authentic leaders, on the other hand, are relatively transparent in expressing their true emotions and feelings to followers, while simultaneously regulating such emotions to minimize any display of inappropriate or potentially damaging emotions. This leads on to a debate about the extent to which leaders can feel secure in displaying emotions. Turnbull James and Arroba argue that 'emotion and emotionality in the system of leadership is complex paradoxical and "hidden beneath the surface" of individuals in ways that do not invite rejection or resistance' (2005, 300).

In summary, focus on the leadership experience offers insights that may support leader development, by acknowledging the significance of trigger events, values and, most importantly, emotions in the leadership process. On the other hand, much more research needs to be conducted with leaders in different industry sectors, cultural contexts and leadership roles in order to translate theories supported by some limited case study research into a more sophisticated framework that will scaffold leaders through environments that involve risk (including the loss of their job), complex relationships, contradictions in expectations of different stakeholders, conflicting value sets and continually evolving organizational environments. Later chapters in this book return to a number of these themes, including: change (Chapter 4), culture and values (Chapter 6) and leadership development (Chapter 7).

REFLECTION The following quotations are from respondents in Turner and Mavin (2006). Comment on whether you are able to identify with one or more of these concerns from your own leadership experience.

> You almost feel that you're in control of your own destiny in terms of managing this business but quite easily somebody with a stroke of a pen could say, we don't need this person anymore

I think we do have to keep performing in this office and I guess that's when I feel most vulnerable. If I spend weeks on a big tender and we don't get it

I feel vulnerable that I might have upset or done something negative without knowing it . . . so I feel vulnerable about unforeseen consequences about what we are doing

Summary and conclusions

This chapter has built on the discussion of leadership style in the previous chapter to explore the impact of context on leadership style, and to introduce some of the most recent thinking about leadership and leadership practice and experience.

Tannenbaum and Schmidt proposed one of the first contingency theories of leadership, with their leadership behaviour continuum. They argued that the most suitable leadership behaviour depended on forces in the management, forces in the subordinates, and forces in the situation. Fielder followed with work that sought to provide a systematic approach to diagnosing the contextual factors that might influence effective leadership style; on this basis he identified three conditions under which a leader might have to work. These vary in terms of the level of structure of the task, the leader's position power, and the relationships between subordinates and the boss. Situational leadership, developed by Hersey and Blanchard, characterized leadership style in terms of the guidance and support that a leader provided; they proposed a model with four basic leadership styles: telling, selling, participating and delegating. They suggested that the choice between these styles should be based on 'follower readiness'. Finally, Goleman has recently proposed the following leadership styles, and made suggestions as to when each was appropriate: coercive, authoritative, affiliative, democratic, pacesetting and coaching. Goleman argued that an effective leader had a portfolio of leadership styles and was able to switch between those styles smoothly and sensitively.

Transformational leadership offers some useful perspectives on the leadership behaviours that might inspire and motivate others. It has been developed alongside models of dispersed leadership which propose the development of leadership capacity throughout the organization.

The final section of this chapter introduced some research into the practice and experience of leadership. Research on leadership in practice moves us forward from notions of what a leader should be like to the practical issues of promoting and cultivating leadership in organizations. This encourages reflection on the difference between leadership emergence and leadership effectiveness, and in particular highlights the very real difficulties associated with developing a shared notion of what constitutes an effective leader, as different stakeholders may have different perspectives. The concept of leadership competencies is a useful tool in the journey to measuring effectiveness, and other factors such as the link between leader behaviours and personality and motivation. Focus on the leadership experience offers insights that may support leader development, by acknowledging the significance of trigger events, values and, most importantly, emotions in the leadership process.

Review questions

1   Outline the contribution that Tannenbaum and Schmidt's continuum of leadership behaviour made to leadership theory.
2   Compare and contrast the factors that situational leadership and Fiedler suggest are important in determining the most effective leadership style. Comment on any differences between these two theories.
3   Discuss situational leadership's notion of follower readiness and its consequences for leadership approaches.
4   Give a specific example of when it might be appropriate to use each of the following of Goleman's leadership styles: coercive, coaching, and affiliative.
5   What are the limitations and criticisms of contingency theories of leadership?
6   Outline the difference between a transformational and a transactional leader.
7   Explain the differences between the concepts 'new leader' and 'super leader'.
8   What do you understand by the term 'leadership competence'? What

has research that focuses on leadership in practice to say?

9 Why is it useful for leadership theories to consider the leadership experience? What dimensions of the leadership experience might it be useful to understand?

Challenges

1 Can leaders change their styles to fit the context, or does a person's personality predispose them to a certain leadership style?

2 How can academics and practitioners arrive at a general purpose model of the different leadership styles that should be in a leader's portfolio?

3 What are the most important factors in the context that should influence leadership style?

4 How can we judge whether a specific leadership style is effective in any specific context?

5 How can leaders retain the trust and confidence of their followers if they switch leadership style to match context?

6 Is a twin track approach that both develops dispersed leadership capacity and supports the emergence of new transformational leaders possible?

7 What do we really understand by the concept leadership effectiveness, and how can it be measured?

8 How can case study based research that offers insights on the leadership experience be used to offer insights into leadership that are useful to leaders and organizations more generally?

Case study interview with Perri-Lee Sandell and Susan Vickery, Managers (job share), Liaison and Research Services (Science), Library Services, Macquarie University, Sydney, Australia

Biographies

Susan graduated from university with a science degree and started working in university libraries then decided to study for a postgraduate diploma in Information

Sciences. She then moved to a medical library role. After seven years (and one child) she returned to work in an academic library as the Science/Faculty Librarian. After her second child she decided to work part time, in a job share with Perri-Lee. Two years later they successfully applied to job share the position of department manager and then followed this with another acting position as Manager, Library Development (responsibilities included staff development, training, communication and partnerships). Susan also attended the Aurora Leadership Institute during this time so became more focused on increasing the capabilities of the library staff. After this she was appointed to her current position as Manager, Liaison & Research Services (Sciences) – a new role created by a restructure.

Perri-Lee has 18 years' experience working in public, special (banking and finance) and academic libraries. She has spent most of her career working in reference and has a keen interest in virtual reference services, developing the first Australian VOIP online reference service 'Ask A Librarian' in 2000. She has job shared three different management roles at Macquarie University Library and is currently Manager, Liaison & Research Services (another job share). She has co-authored and presented three papers, most recently on attracting and retaining Generation Y to the library and information science profession (with Susan Vickery).

1 Do you believe that different leadership styles are appropriate in different circumstances?

Perri-Lee: Yes, I believe in situational leadership, depending on the circumstances, if there is a task or project that needs to be done. If I have someone who is willing and able I can delegate the task. If someone is willing but not up to speed or less capable, I may need to coach them and provide a greater amount of direction and support.

Susan: Definitely! One of the themes I was trying to pick up on at the recent IFLA satellite conference on leadership development was the cultural differences in leadership styles and differences in reception to leadership style . . . particularly relevant for multicultural societies. Not just cultural differences but also individual differences. You really need to be in touch with the values and needs of those you are trying to influence (or lead) otherwise you end up banging against a wall. Sometimes you may need to be more assertive, sometimes more inspirational. It's also a matter of tuning in to people's motivators.

2 Do you feel that you are able to adapt your leadership style to the circumstances?

Perri-Lee: I do feel that I am able to adapt my leadership style. I think I am a psychological leader as I often play the part of counsellor. I find people are comfortable coming to me asking me what I think they should do in a particular situation. Over the years I have had individuals ask my opinion on how they should talk to their peers about a difficult issue and I have also had people ask me how they should approach their manager. Although I am a psychological leader most of the time I know when I need to bring out the effective or responsible leader in myself.

Susan: I have to admit that this does not always come naturally to me, and that sometimes I have to sit back and ponder why I'm not having the desired effect. Normally it's because I need to recognize that this person is coming from a different angle, and so I need to adapt my leadership style to suit. Something I'm still working on . . . aren't we all???

3 Has your leadership style changed over the years? If so, how?

Perri-Lee: I still lean towards a coaching/mentoring style of leadership. I enjoy developing others. My style has changed only in the fact that I have become more firm in my beliefs and have strength in my convictions. Early in my career I wanted to please everyone with my decisions, now I have learnt that to be an effective, respected leader one doesn't have to be liked. I have realized that as a leader it is far more important to 'listen' and 'act'.

Susan: Before taking on any type of officially recognized 'managerial position' I was definitely in awe of the role and assumed that good managers needed to have some special gift or deep understanding that made them know what to do in any situation. We all have worked with 'bad managers' who have lacked this and I didn't want to be one myself. It was actually my brother who convinced me that this was not the case. In fact I had been a 'leader' many times over in different roles both personal and professional – but had not recognized this.

I used to assume that as my style was not the same as someone else's, then that was a weakness on my behalf. One of my 'aha' moments at the Aurora Leadership Institute was recognising different styles of leadership and that my style had its own strengths (and weaknesses). One of my personal challenges is building up my confidence in my own opinions and so speak up more. I also use my relationship with my team to help me recognize what my manager/supervisor etc. is expecting from me.

4 What actions do you take to promote dispersed leadership in your organization?

Perri-Lee: I often approach others to 'go for' a project or opportunity that they may not have considered so they can 'dip their toe in the water' and develop their potential as a leader, thus seeing if they enjoy the experience.

Susan: I encourage everyone to speak up on what they believe. In our team meetings we encourage discussion of issues and try to be more 'hands-off' so that people are encouraged to make decisions for themselves and be accountable. As a Generation X-er I am all for accountability at all levels and struggle with displays of martyr type behaviour as well as helplessness, i.e. 'What's the point in speaking up – no one is listening', 'there is already an agenda', 'I could have told you it wasn't going to work', etc. We try to get the rumblings out in the open so that there can be an honest evaluation of the issue.

I also try to involve my discussion of issues with all levels of staff (not just with managers). I think this shows the individual at all levels that their knowledge is valued and in turn encourages their continued input – not to mention that they normally have a different (and sometimes more accurate) perspective of what is going on!

5 Can you give an example of an incident when different stakeholders (e.g. peers, subordinates and line managers) might have judged your leadership effectiveness differently? How did you manage this situation?

Perri-Lee: A few years ago, I was acting managing for my department and I was facilitating the managing change process. My previous peers became my subordinates. I needed to demonstrate a consultative style of leadership. This was particularly difficult for one of my peers as she would have preferred me to use a participative style of leadership. My line manager expected me to be tough and not so 'emotional' to my peers wants/needs. The experience taught me that being transparent and listening to feedback doesn't mean that you need to agree with the demands that are being placed on you.

Susan: Whilst working on our draft restructure proposal for the department – acting as Departmental Manager – our staff (who were also our peers once the 'acting was finished') wanted us to be more consultative and inclusive in our leadership. At the same time we were perhaps lacking in confidence in our ability as we were 'only acting in the position'. The management team was telling us to keep to a deadline, make a call, and be more directive. Some in the department thought we were being 'puppets' to management, others thought we were being unconsultative. It was a very challenging time for me, as the differing parties had very different expectations about how we should be working. In the end we had to do what we thought best, which meant not everybody was happy. We either consulted too much, or too little, depending on their perspective.

6 Has there been a trigger event in your life that has changed your attitude to leadership? What happened and how has it affected you?

Perri-Lee: Yes there was an event that made me question my confidence in myself as a leader. At a week long intensive professional development course I challenged myself that I was too confident in my ability to lead. After my initial doubt I came to realize that confidence is a good quality not a bad one.

Susan: One key event was recognizing that leadership does not necessarily equal 'manager' and that you can lead from behind as well as from the front. I think my response to Question 3 sort of sums this up. Also at Aurora a group of mentors honestly spoke of a time in their life when they had a leadership 'crisis' and how they dealt with it. That was when I realized that I didn't have to have all the answers. Also I learnt to value my style of leadership.

7 How do you manage leadership in a job sharing role?

Perri-Lee: I stay true to my own personal style and don't try to be something I'm not. By nature Susan and I are yin and yang – with different strengths and weaknesses. We feel our colleagues get the best of both worlds with us! Having said this we are consistent in the key areas – we see communication as paramount as well as the need to inspire others with our vision/strategy and develop them so that they can perform at their best.

Susan: Despite the fact that we can finish each other's sentences, we are quite different in our strengths so we find that we naturally lead each other, acting as mentors. We are big communicators and also very honest, even saying when we think the other could have handled a situation better, or alternatively openly admiring the way the other may have dealt with something. I feel I have learnt so much more being in this relationship, which is why I'm such a supporter of it as a tool for development. We also give each other the room to grow . . . so we can branch off into areas we are more attracted to.

In relation to the team we manage, we spend a lot of our cross-over time discussing the development of individuals and make a big effort to be consistent in the messages we send to our staff.

References and additional reading

Adair, J. (1979) *Action-centred Leadership*, Aldershot, Gower.

Adair, J. (2007) *How to Grow Leaders*, London, Kogan Page.

Alimo-Metcalfe, B. and Alban-Metcalfe, J. (2002) The Great and the Good, *People Management*, **8** (11), 32–4.

Alimo-Metcalfe, B. and Alban-Metcalfe, J. (2003) Under the Influence, *People and Management*, **9** (5), 32–5.

Alimo-Metcalfe, B. and Alban-Metcalfe, J. (2005) Leadership: time for a new direction?, *Leadership*, **1** (1), 51–71.

Allredge, M. E. and Nilan, K. J. (2000) 3M's Leadership Competency Model: an internally developed solution, *Human Resources Management*, **39** (2–3), 133–45.

Barling, J., Slater, F. and Kelloway, E. K. (2000) Transformational Leadership and Emotional Intelligence: an exploratory study, *Leadership & Organization Development Journal*, **21** (3), 157–61.

Bartram, D. (2005) The Great Eight Competencies: a criterion-centric approach to validation, *Journal of Applied Psychology*, **90**, 1185–203.

Bartram, D. and Brown, A. (2006) Leadership Emergence and Leadership Approval: an evidence-based approach, *Proceedings of the British*

Academy of Management, September 2006, Belfast.

Bartram, D., Robertson, I. T. and Callinan, M. (2002) Introduction: a framework for examining organizational effectiveness. In Robertson, T., Callinan, M. and Bartram, D. (eds), *Organizational Effectiveness: the role of psychology*, Chichester, Wiley, 1–12.

Bass, B. M. (1990) From Transactional to Transformational Leadership: learning to share the vision, *Organizational Dynamics*, **18** (3), 19–31.

Bass, B. M. (1998) *Transformational Leadership: industry, military and educational impact*, London, Lawrence Earlbaum.

Bass, B. M. and Avolio, B. J. (1990) The Implications of Transactional and Transformational Leadership for Individual, Team and Organizational Development, *Research and Organizational Change and Development*, **4**, 321–72.

Bass, B. M. and Avolio, B. J. (1994) *Improving Organizational Effectiveness Through Transformational Leadership*, Thousand Oaks, CA, Sage.

Bennis, W. and Nanus, B. (1985) *Leaders: the strategies for taking charge,* New York, Harper.

Burns, J. M. (1978) *Leadership*, New York, Harper and Row.

Castiglione, J. (2006) Organizational Learning and Transformational Leadership in the Library Environment, *Library Management*, **27** (4/5), 289–99.

Chen, J.-C. and Silverstone, C. (2005) Leadership Effectiveness, Leadership Style and Employee Readiness, *Leadership & Organization Development Journal*, **26** (4), 280–8.

Clarke, C. and Pratt, S. (1985) Leadership's Four-part Progress, *Management Today*, March, 84–6.

Cole, G. A. (2004) *Management Theory and Practice*, 6th edn, London, Thomson.

Debowski, S. (2006) *Knowledge Management*, Sydney, Wiley, Chapter 3.

Fielder, F. E. (1967) *A Theory of Leadership Effectiveness*, New York, McGraw-Hill.

Gardner, W. L., Avolio, B. J., Luthans, F., May, D. R. and Walumbra, F. (2005) Can You See the Real Me? A self based model of authentic leader and follower development, *The Leadership Quarterly*, **16**, 343–72.

Gill, R. (2006) *Theory and Practice of Leadership*, London, Sage Publications.

Goleman, D. (2000) Leadership That Gets Results, *Harvard Business Review*, **78** (2), 78–90.

Goleman, R. E., Boyatzis, E. and McKee, A. (2002) *The New Leader: transforming the art of leadership into the science of results*, Boston, Little, Brown.

Heifetz, R. A. and Laurie, D. L. (1997) The 'Work of Leadership', *Harvard Business Review*, **75** (1), 809–37.

Hersey, P. and Blanchard, K. H. (1988) Management of Organizational Behavior: utilizing human resources, 5th edn, Englewood Cliffs, NJ, Prentice-Hall.

Hogan, R. and Kasier, R. B. (2005) What We Know About Leadership, *Review of General Psychology*, **9**, 169–80.

Hollenback, G. P., McCall, M. W. and Silzer, R. F. (2006) Leadership Competency Models, *The Leadership Quarterly*, **17**, 398–413.

Luthans, F. and Avolio, B. J. (2003) Authentic Leadership: a positive development approach. In Cameron, K. S., Dutton, J. E. and Quinn, R. E. (eds), *Positive Organizational Scholarship*, San Francisco, Barrett-Koehler, 241–61.

Mintzberg, H. (1998) Covert Leadership: notes on managing professionals; knowledge workers respond to inspiration, not supervision, *Harvard Business Review*, **76** (6), 140–7.

Mitchie, S. and Gooty, J. (2005) Values, Emotions and Authenticity: will the real leaders please stand up, *The Leadership Quarterly*, **16** (3), 441–57.

Mullins, L. J. (2005) *Management and Organizational Behaviour*, 7th edn, Harlow, FT Prentice Hall.

Parry, K. W. and Bryan, A. (2006) Leadership in Organizations. In Clegg, S. R., Hardy, C., Lawrence, T. and Nord, W. R. (eds), *The Sage Handbook of Organization Studies*, 2nd edn, London, Sage Publications.

Politis, J. D. (2001) The Relationship of Various Leadership Styles to Knowledge Management, *Leadership & Organization Development Journal*, **22** (8), 354–64.

Rodrigues, C. A.)(1988) Identifying the Right Leader for the Right Situation, *Personnel*, September, 43–6.

Rodrigues, C. A. (1993) Developing Three-dimensional Leaders, *Journal of Management Development*, **12** (3), 4–iv.

Shao, L. and Webber, S. (2006) A Cross-cultural Test of the 'Five Factor Model of Personality and Transformational Leadership', *Journal of Business Research*, **59**, 936–44.

Storey, J. (ed.) (2004) *Leadership in Organizations: current issues and key trends*, London, Routledge.

Tannenbaum, R. and Schmidt, W. H. (1958) How to Choose a Leadership Pattern, *Harvard Business Review*, **36** (2), 95–102.

Turnbull James, K. and Arroba, T. (2005) Reading and Carrying: a framework for learning about emotion and emotionality in organizational systems as a core aspect of leadership development, *Management Learning*, **36** (3), 299–316.

Turner, J. and Marvin, S. (2006) Authentic Leadership Journeys? Narratives of senior leaders, *Proceedings of the British Academy of Management Conference*, September 2006, Belfast.

Van Wart, M. (2003) Public-sector Leadership Theory: an assessment, *Public Administration Review*, **63** (2), 214–28.

Vera, D. and Crossan, M. (2004) Strategic Leadership and Organizational Learning, *Academy of Management Review*, **29** (2), 222–40.

Vroom, V. H. and Yetton, P. W. (1973) *Leadership and Decision-making*, Pittsburgh, University of Pittsburgh Press.

Williams, M. (2006) *Mastering Leadership*, 2nd edn, London, Thorogood.

Yukl, G. (1998) *Leadership in Organizations*, 4th edn, Englewood Cliffs, NJ, Prentice-Hall.

4

Change and innovation

Learning objectives

After reading this chapter you should be able to:

- ☑ discuss models of change and its processes
- ☑ appreciate people's experience and response to change
- ☑ understand the concept of change leadership
- ☑ discuss the role and characteristics of change agents
- ☑ debate the benefits of the innovation perspective on change.

Introduction

Leadership involves formulating direction and exercising influence to ensure that a team or organization moves forward, and it is therefore inevitable that leadership is associated with change. Leaders need to understand change processes, how to support and engage people through change processes and how to create an organizational culture in which change is not only expected, but welcomed. On a personal level they have to have the confidence to enjoy change even when it is associated with a steep personal learning curve, managing issues that might seem trivial to the bigger picture but which might be important to individuals, rescuing something from frustratingly irresolvable conflicts, and dealing with elaborate bureaucracies. To be inspiring and motivating to others, the leader has to be inspired and motivated themselves. This chapter seeks to offer some concepts, perspectives and models that can be used to promote the effectiveness of change processes.

Change and its processes

There are many different types of change process. Sometimes change is evolutionary and incremental, but on other occasions more radical change is required. Major changes, such as an organizational re-organization, often have significant consequences for employees' roles and jobs; such processes need both leadership and management. Changing marketplace dynamics in the private sector, and shifting political and government agendas in the public sector, coupled with technological innovation and increasing information and knowledge flows in organizations, are all important and continuing drivers for change. Information organizations, being at the heart of the knowledge revolution, have undergone many changes in recent years and there is no reason to believe that the rate of change will slow. Figure 4.1 summarizes some of the triggers for change for information services.

Within the context of academic libraries, Lougee (2002) observes that since research libraries support all sectors of academic life, they are at the nexus of change in higher education. As the information and knowledge revolution has advanced, the roles of academic libraries are changing as they become more deeply engaged in the creation and dissemination of knowledge and increasingly act as key collaborators with the other stakeholders in these activities. The challenge, as for many organizations, is to respond to change while sustaining traditional functions.

Yet, there are impressive examples of change leadership within the information industry. Brindley (2007) discusses the journey to establish the British Library as a world-class institution for the 21st century. She talks about not just adapting to but leading change, and developing new paradigms. This change has involved revolution and modernization of services, and facing up to difficult staff and people issues, but has led to a much higher government and public profile. One of the challenges is working simultaneously on

External triggers of change:
- technological innovation, such as wireless, mobile technologies
- new media formats, such as e-books, RSS news feeds, MP3s
- changes in user/customer information activities and expectations, e.g. e-learning, digital access to information resources
- activities and innovation of other information providers, e.g. national libraries, commercial information providers, internet search engines, and other library and information services
- legislation and government policies, e.g. relating to data protection, freedom of information, and intellectual property rights
- changes in social and cultural values, e.g. in relation to the importance of information and knowledge, and in being well informed
- changes in economic and political regimes, e.g. affecting funding of information services, and pricing and licensing of access to published information resources.

Internal triggers of change:
- development of new services and innovation in service processes
- low staff performance, morale and motivation leading to high stress and staff turnover
- new appointments to senior or pivotal posts
- relocation and buildings development
- restructuring to improve efficiency and effectiveness, leading to reallocation of roles, and often a need for training and development.

Figure 4.1 Some typical triggers of change for information services

different planes, on global and local solutions, balancing traditional roles of collection and stewardship while at the same time trying to map digital publishing. Winston (2005) draws attention to the incidence and practice of library leadership in the broader social contexts, particularly during a period of crisis or change, such as during wars, social movements, healthcare crises, and large-scale economic and technological shifts. Although this impressive review is a reminder of the contributions that libraries can make to communities and organizations in turbulent times, such contributions involve the wider leadership that is discussed further in the final chapter, but also imply significant and sometimes rapid change within the information organization. On the other hand, while these authors reflect on the 'big' picture, there is also a need to consider change in specific contexts. For example, Siddiqui (2003) discusses the management of change for acquisitions departments in academic libraries. The management of change, like leadership, is not only the prerogative of the library or information services director, but involves everybody.

Various authors remind us that many change initiatives fail to achieve substantial and lasting results (Kotter, 1995; Smith, 2006). For a number of reasons even capable and well-intentioned people can make predictable mistakes when they attempt to progress substantial change, hence the importance of change leadership. Earlier in this book (Chapter 2) we started to explore the difference between management and leadership; this is a topic that it is useful to revisit specifically in the context of change. Kotter (1999) makes the differentiation between management and leadership; he suggests that management is about coping with complexity, while leadership is about coping with change. Managers focus on the capacity of the organization to achieve its goals by organizing and staffing. In contrast, the focus for leadership is the communication of the new direction to those who will be instrumental in creating coalitions that can understand the vision and are committed to its achievement. Thus managers work by controlling and problem-solving; leaders succeed by motivating and inspiring. More change requires more leadership, and increasingly managers are also required to be leaders, but as we have discussed earlier, leadership roles may also be fulfilled by those who are not designated as managers, on the basis of their relevant expertise and roles. Riggs (2001) agrees that the library manager focuses on the means to an end, whereas the library leader is entrepreneurial with a vision for the library, and a focus on how that vision can be achieved.

One of the very early and widely known models of the change process was Lewin's (1951) unfreeze, move and refreeze model. This model assumes that change is a response to a specific trigger, such as one of the external or internal triggers listed in Figure 4.1. According to Lewin, the change process involves unfreezing the current situation through consultation and communication; transforming it, for example, by introducing new technology, work processes, services and so on; and refreezing so that the new technology, work processes or services become the steady state and familiar. However, change is not usually as straightforward as Lewin's simple model suggests for the following reasons:

1   Often the triggers for change are interlinked. For information services, for example, the introduction of the internet has affected social and cultural attitudes to information access, provided new formats for

information delivery, and changed users' expectation of an information service.

2   Although some triggers for change, such as the appointment of a new member of staff to a senior position, occur at a specific point in time, many more triggers act in an evolutionary manner. For example, the digitization of information resources has been under way for decades, yet within this arena there continue to be specific initiatives, projects and technological innovation that might herald significant change for some information services.

3   Organizational change impacts differently at individual, group and organizational levels, so it is important to study and manage change at each of these levels separately, but also to be sensitive to the interactions between levels. Pettigrew (1985, 1987) suggests that there are many interrelated factors that influence the nature and outcomes of change. He suggests that change is a cocktail of rational decisions competing with individual perceptions, visionary leadership, power play and attempts to recruit and support coalitions. Dawson (2003) suggests that in order to understand organizational change processes it is necessary to take into account:

— the past, present and future context in which the organization functions (including internal and external triggers as discussed earlier)
— the nature or substance of the change itself
— the transition process, including tasks, activities, decision, timing and sequencing
— political activity
— interaction between these factors.

4   Change is a process that takes time and resources. Information systems developers sometimes forget this when they install a new system that affects work processes; there is a temptation for them to assume that once the system is 'up and running' and staff have been trained in system use, that the change has been completed. This is unlikely to be the case, since training is typically followed by a longer period during which staff learn how to integrate the system into their working processes and practices. These 'adoption' stages are an important part of

the change process. Accordingly different stakeholders may have different views on the length of a change process, and this can pose challenges in the analysis and monitoring of such processes.

5   Change and cultures, as discussed in chapter 6 are tightly interwoven (see Chapter 6). Any change will affect culture and culture will influence the nature and process of a change process (Naylor, 2004).

Thus change management theorists suggest that organizations are in a continuous state of flux, and that change processes are complex and difficult to analyse, influence and manage. Much of the remainder of this chapter focuses on how leaders and managers can take steps to ensure they achieve more effective and successful outcomes from change interventions. However, before moving on to focus on the management of change, it is important to remember that not all things change and not all types of change are 'good'. Specifically it is important to remember:

◆   to *take a holistic perspective* and understand change in relation to those things that remain constant over time and through change processes; continuity may be equally as important as change, and successful change interventions are often achieved by balancing change with stability

◆   that too much change leads to *initiative decay* where the benefits of previous change are lost because the organization moves on rapidly to another change cycle, thereby making it difficult to bed in and evaluate new processes and their associated impact on performance

◆   that too much change may also lead to *initiative fatigue*, in which people who have experienced too many change initiatives become tired of and resistant to change. Toffler (1970) believes that there is a limit to the amount of change individuals can handle. Too much change in too short a time provokes stress and disorientation. In particular a stable mission, in the midst of considerable structural and operational change, can form a valuable anchor. For example, the British Library continues to be committed to the original mission, framed in 1753, by the founders who built up its contributing collections, which was to make the resources freely available 'for all posterity', providing access to the world's knowledge for 'all studious and curious persons' (Brindley, 2007).

REFLECTION Make a list of the things (e.g. people, tasks, roles, stories, reputation, physical environment) that have not changed in your information organization in the last ten years. If you have not been in the organization for ten years, ask someone who has.

Successful change management needs to balance a response to external and internal triggers for change with stability and continuity in order to avoid initiative decay and fatigue. In other words, however attractive it might appear to a manager or leader in terms of personal career and ego to engage in unnecessary and disruptive change, striking the balance between change and continuity is likely to be the most successful in the longer term.

Abrahamson (2000) suggests that change management should involve 'dynamic stability', in which change involves carefully paced major initiatives (called kludging), interspersed with periods of smaller change (called tinkering). Collins' model (cited in Huczynski and Buchanan, 2007, 591), which discusses the nature of the change management task in terms of the extent and impact of the change under consideration, offers a further perspective to assist in balancing change with stability and continuity. Collins proposes that changes can range from shallow (fine tuning), with a focus on efficiency, through stages that involve restructuring, resource reallocation and leadership change, to deep (change the mission, vision, values and philosophy) and deepest (paradigm shift with fundamental change in perspective, position, behaviour and strategy). A key issue is that in most organizations change with different time frames and at different levels of depth are typically ongoing at the same time.

Change in organizations is complex and the change leader's main prerogative must be that of sense-maker. The change leader needs to help others to understand the organization and their continuing contribution to that organization. This commences with convincing people that they have a contribution to make, and then moves on to motivating, enabling and empowering them to make that contribution, and acknowledging their achievements along the way. Central to change leadership is the 'management of meaning', including 'selling' particular perspectives on problems and solutions in order to gain compliance and assent.

People and change

People respond to change in different ways. This section first continues and extends the discussion of the link between change and stress. Then the coping cycle model is used as a framework for considering emotional responses to the change experience. Finally, the recognition that change is not always a positive experience leads to a discussion of the reasons for resistance to change and the techniques for responding to it.

The Yerkes–Dodson (1908) hypothesis considers the relationship between pressure (or stress) levels experienced by people and their performance. As shown in Table 4.1, the Yerkes–Dodson hypothesis suggests that for most people there is an optimum level of stress or pressure to achieve optimum performance. If pressure is too low, people are bored and deliver only acceptable performance; on the other hand, too extreme pressure levels lead to panic and the consequence is once again low performance. Optimum performance is associated with a moderate level of pressure or stress. A leader's role is to understand and monitor the optimum stress levels of specific individuals in order to ensure optimum performance. There are a number of signs that indicate when people are under more stress than they are comfortable with. These include unexplained absences, high sickness rates, declining interpersonal relationships, accidents and mistakes, being the subject of customer complaints, and employee grievances.

Table 4.1 The Yerkes–Dodson hypothesis on the pressure–performance relationship (based on Huczynski and Buchanan, 2007)

Pressure level	Response	Performance
Very low	Boredom	Low to acceptable
Low to moderate	Comfort	Moderate to high
Moderate to high	Stretch	High, above expectations
High to unrealistic	Stress	Moderate to low
Extreme	Panic	Low, unacceptable

Drawing on studies of how we cope with traumatic personal loss, Kubler-Ross (1969) proposed that we deal with loss by moving through a series of emotional stages, described as the 'coping cycle' (see Table 4.2). Not all changes that people experience in the workplace will be experienced as loss, and some of those that are will be seen as a mild loss which might only invoke a negligible emotional response. On the other hand, some changes, such as a new job, redundancy, a new boss, a new time-keeping regime or the introduction of a new computer system, will involve loss, though they may also provide new opportunities. Although each individual responds differently to change situations, there are times when people benefit from being supported through the coping cycle, by being given space to experience emotions and to come to terms with moving forward.

Table 4.2 The coping cycle

Stage	Response
Denial	Unwillingness to accept the reality
Anger	Directing accusation to those perceived to be responsible
Bargaining	Attempts to negotiate and mitigate loss
Depression	Recognition that loss or transition is real and dealing with its consequences
Acceptance	Coming to terms with the situation and seeking way to move forward

Recognition that individuals do not always perceive change to be in their own interest is an important aspect of leading people through change processes. When people cannot see the benefit of change they are likely to resist it. The factors that might lead to a resistance to change include:

◆ *vested interests*, based on seeking to protect a favourable status quo
◆ *fear and anxiety*, fuelled, for instance, by misunderstanding and lack of trust, as when people do not understand the need for a change, its nature or its possible consequences
◆ *lack of clarity* about the objectives for and nature of change, leading to contradictory assessment in which individuals view the change situation differently, depending on their position and personal values
◆ *low tolerance for change*, because some people have a low tolerance for ambiguity and uncertainty; change potentially challenges their self-concept (see Chapter 2) and often invalidates hard learnt skills and competencies.

REFLECTION Make a list of the things that you would miss if a major restructure led to you being relocated to a different work group with a slightly different role, but on the same grade as at present.

It is important to recognize that not all resistance to change is at the individual or group level. Mullins (2007) talks about organizational resistance to change. He suggests that in order to ensure operational effectiveness, organizations often set up defences against change and prefer to focus on the routine things that they have learnt to perform well; this is the mirror of the individual who resists change because it challenges their opportunity to exercise their skills and competencies. Some of the main reasons for organizational resistance to change are:

◆ *organizational culture*, which typically has a strong legacy component
◆ the need to maintain *stability* and *predictability*, which is often seen as important for ensuring that large organizations work effectively; change in one part of an organization has consequences elsewhere in the organization
◆ the *cost* of investing in new resources – change often requires resources, and usually organizational resources are committed, and assets such as buildings, technology, equipment and people cannot be easily changed; for example, a branch library with a location that is no longer in a centre of a community may have difficulty re-locating
◆ the effect of *past contracts* or agreements with other parties such as suppliers and customers, which are very rigid; in information services, photocopier contracts are notoriously restrictive of change
◆ *threats to power* or influence of specific groups or departments; for example, library managers may resist providing open access to information for their staff over the intranet because this may be viewed as bypassing their authority.

Often those managing change need not only to counter any resistance to change, but also to manage the politics of change. Most change situations are opportunities for different stakeholder groups to seek to protect or further their own interests. Those individuals and groups who perceive their interests to be threatened are likely to resist change, while those who see opportunities for advancing their interests are likely to embrace change. The leader's role is to do their best to negotiate a win–win outcome, which is positive for as many stakeholders as possible, whilst simultaneously achieving the overall performance objectives of the organization. Cunningham (2005) maintains that it is a myth that people resist change, and suggests that people love change, provided that they do not perceive a future loss.

Mutula (2000) discusses how an inclusive consultative approach was used to reconcile stakeholders' divergent beliefs, interests and aspirations during change at the United States International University Library in Kenya.

REFLECTION What are the stakeholder groups that might be affected by a change in a resource centre opening hours? What are their interests with respect to this change?

Kotter and Schlesinger (1979) identified six techniques for responding to any potential resistance to change:

◆ *education and commitment* – ensuring that managers share their perceptions, knowledge and objectives through communication and training
◆ *participation and involvement* – involving those who might resist change in the planning of change, and thereby encouraging commitment
◆ *facilitation and support* – supporting employees in managing their response to and fears of change
◆ *negotiation and agreement* – to reach a mutually agreeable compromise to accommodate the interest of powerful resistors
◆ *manipulation and co-optation* – covert attempts to sidestep potential resistance, through proposals that deliberately respond to specific interests and sensitivities
◆ *implicit and explicit coercion* – in the face of irresolvable differences, change leaders may resort to force and threat.

The first three of the above techniques – education and commitment, participation and involvement, and facilitation and support – are designed to create an environment that will minimize the chance of parochial self-interest, misunderstanding and contradictory assessments occuring. The final three techniques – negotiation and agreement, manipulation and co-optation, and implicit and explicit coercion – are approaches to managing the espoused difference in interests between different stakeholder groups.

Instead of offering a range of approaches to change management, Pettinger (2007), identifies the following keys to effective and sustainable change:

◆ *integrity and directness*
◆ *clarity of purpose*, strategy, directional priority, easily understood by all affected
◆ *clarity of communication*
◆ *clear monitoring*, review and evaluation processes, so that problems and teething troubles are addressed as soon as they become apparent
◆ *consultation, counselling and support* for individuals and groups that know, believe or perceive themselves to be at risk
◆ *a trouble-shooting* capacity for addressing problems and issues as they arise.

Often a change situation calls for the use of several of Kotter and Schlesinger's approaches and attention to most of Pettinger's keys in combination. This need to balance collaboration, consultation, direction and coercion has been re-visited more recently by Stace and Dunphy (2001), as discussed in the next section.

An overarching model of change management into which many of these approaches and considerations can be integrated is force field analysis. In force field analysis, forces driving change and those restraining change are separated out, and attention is directed towards strengthening driving forces and removing or neutralizing restraining forces. Driving forces might, for example, be strengthened through consultation and communication, while restraining forces might be reduced by negotiation, agreement, facilitation and support.

Change leadership

The previous two sections have established that change and change processes are complex, and that people's response to change is variable. In response to this, during the 20th century there has been general agreement that employee participation is central to engendering a positive response to change. On the other hand, there is a growing recognition that participation and its associated processes are time consuming and that there are some differences in the interests of the stakeholders within an organization that simply cannot be reconciled. Dunphy and Stace (1990; Stace and Dunphy, 2001) suggest that the optimum leadership style depends on the scale of change. They propose a contingency model with four different types of leadership that align with different styles of change leadership, as shown in Tables 4.3 and 4.4.

Table 4.3 Dunphy and Stace's contingent change leadership styles

	Incremental change strategies	**Transformative change strategies**
Collaborative–consultative modes	**Participative evolution** Suitable for minor adjustment where time is available and where key interest groups can be brought on board	**Charismatic transformation** Suitable for major adjustments, where there is little time for participation and where there is support for radical change
Directive–coercive modes	**Forced evolution** Suitable for minor adjustment, where time is available, but key interest groups oppose change	**Dictatorial transformation** Suitable for major adjustments where there is no time for participation and where there is no internal support for major change that is necessary for survival

Table 4.4 Change leaders for Dunphy and Stace's 'Huc and Buc' change leadership styles

Type of change leadership style	**Type of change leader**	**Description**
Participative	Coaches	People-centred, inspirational, communicators
Forced evolution	Captains	Systematic, task-oriented authority figures
Charismatic transformation	Charismatics	'Heroic' figures who are able to sell their own dramatic and challenging vision to others and carry others with them
Dictatorial transformation	Commanders	Purposeful, decisive, tough-minded, forceful, with an ability to neutralize or remove resistance

REFLECTION 'Commanders' are often recruited from outside the organization. Why do you think that this might be?

Dunphy and Stace's work aligns with the contingency theories of leadership discussed in Chapter 3, and raises similar questions. For example, is it possible for leaders to adapt their leadership style to suit different conditions, or do people have a preferred style, based on their personality? Further, if people do change their style, does this provoke a crisis of trust, because followers no longer have a sense that they know the person? Such speculations lead in turn to the question as to whether the same person can effectively lead both incremental and transformational change.

Change agents

The previous section discussed the idea of change leadership style; this concept is complemented by the concept of the change agent, those individuals within organizations who seek to promote, further, support, sponsor, initiate, implement or help to deliver change. Change agents may be managers or specialize in the substance of the change, such as IT specialists. The change agent may be the person who feels that change is necessary, someone charged with making a change happen, or consultants who specialize in change management. Good change agents are able to combine appropriate technical or business expertise with interpersonal and managerial skills. Kanter (1989) identifies the following key skills of a change agent:

◆ being able to work independently, without management power, sanction or support
◆ being an effective collaborator
◆ being able to develop high trust relationships, based on high ethical standards
◆ having self-confidence tempered with humility
◆ showing respect for both the process and content of change
◆ being able to work across business functions and units
◆ being willing to stake rewards on results and to gain satisfaction from success.

Innovation, not change

Discussion of change management tends to rest on the assumption that change leaders and change agents either know what change is necessary, or are able, through collaboration and consultation, to arrive at a compromise that specifies what needs to happen. Innovation literature makes a contribution by focusing on the processes associated with the development of the innovation in processes and products that are necessary in order to ensure continuing success for the organization. In today's organizational environments innovation and the development of new ideas, devices, systems, processes, products or services need to be ongoing. Leaders need to be continually monitoring for and engaging in potential improvements, developments and enhancements in all aspects of their organizations. Riggs (1989) is a significant, if somewhat dated, collection, which emphasizes the importance of creativity, innovation and entrepreneurship in libraries.

Christensen and Overdorf (2000) distinguish between *sustaining innovations*, which improve existing products and services, and *disruptive innovations*, which involve the development of completely new processes, procedures, services and products. Although many key innovations relate to products and services, *operational innovations*, which focus on work processes, can have a significant effect on efficiency and effectiveness. Sharing of best practice can be particularly significant in driving operational innovation, but it is important to remember that practices often need to be adapted to fit circumstances.

Various authors have suggested that some organizations encourage innovation, while others stifle innovation and creativity, and encourage risk avoidance (Kanter, 1989; Ekvall, 1996; Ekvall and Ryhammer, 1999). Ekvall (1996) and Ekvall and Ryhammer (1999) proposed the concept of the creative organization climate. This climate has ten dimensions, as shown in Table 4.5, each of which can be managed to promote or inhibit innovation.

Recent work from the Advanced Institute of Management Research with the Chartered Management Institute focuses on the role of leaders in innovation (AIMR, 2005). This research suggests that leaders have a dual role in innovation:

◆   as *motivators*, inspiring people to transcend the ordinary

◆ as *architects*, designing an organizational environment that enables employees to be innovative.

The research distinguishes between leaders who primarily motivate through transformational actions (motivators) and those who have a more transactional approach, which focuses on the co-ordination of organizational tasks (architects).

Table 4.5 The creative organization climate (Ekvall, 1996; Ekvall and Ryhammer, 1999)

Dimension	For promotion of innovation
Challenge	People experience challenge, joy and meaning in work
Freedom	People make contacts, give and receive information freely, discuss problems, make decisions, take initiatives
Idea support	Ideas and suggestions are received in a supportive way by bosses and colleagues
Trust/openness	Ideas can be expressed without fear of reprisal or ridicule; communications are open
Dynamism/liveliness	New things happen all of the time
Playfulness/humour	Relaxed atmosphere with jokes and laughter
Debates	Many voices are heard expressing different ideas and viewpoints
Conflicts	Conflicts of ideas not people
Risk taking	Decisions and actions prompt and rapid
Idea time	Opportunities to discuss and test fresh ideas that are not part of planned work activity

REFLECTION Examine Table 4.5 and discuss the extent to which the organization in which you work has a creative organization climate. To what extent do you think that the dimensions of the creative organization climate are inter-related with each other?

While Ekvall and others have focused on the organizational climate for innovation, Pinchot (1984) focused on individuals as innovators. Pinchot proposed the term 'intrapreneur' to describe enterprising individuals working within organizations. Intrapreneurs can be important nodes of innovation within organizations, provided that the organization climate supports their creativity, invention and innovation. Pinchot's ten commandments (Figure 4.2) suggest that too often intrapreneurs may be at odds with the general organizational conditions. Intrapreneurs are capable of turning ideas into action. They seek the opportunity to empower others, draw them into their sphere of influence, let them make their own mistakes, and use these as a vehicle for collective and individual development. Such approaches and attitudes may be counter to the normal power structure in the organization and are not always easy to reconcile with the regular activities of the organization.

Many leaders in non-management positions in information services are likely to be intrapreneurs. Such individuals may also be the leaders of the future. They have important contributions to make in improving performance, but they may not always 'obey all of the rules'. Information service managers, and leaders with formal responsibility for driving change and innovation in the organization, need to develop strategies for accommodating and encouraging intrapreneurs and, more generally, creativity across the organization. Reflection on the dimensions of a creative organizational climate is a good place to start.

1	Come to work each day willing to be fired.
2	Circumvent any orders aimed at stopping your dream.
3	Do any job needed to make your project work, regardless of your job description.
4	Find people to help you.
5	Follow your intuition about the people you choose and work only with the best.
6	Work underground as long as you can – publicity triggers the corporate immune system.
7	Never bet on a race unless you are running in it.
8	Remember that it is easer to ask for forgiveness than for permission.
9	Be true to your goals and be realistic about the way you achieve them.
10	Keep your sponsors informed.

Figure 4.2 The intrapreneur's ten commandments (Pinchot, 1984)

REFLECTION What kinds of problems do you think that an intrapreneur operating to Pinchot's 'ten commandments' might pose for management in your information organization?

Summary and conclusions

Leading change is a key aspect of leadership. It requires attention to many of the issues that have been addressed in the earlier chapter of this book, such as supporting teams to work together, adopting an appropriate leadership style, being aware of and intervening in culture, and setting direction. Change management theorists, however, have developed a range of concepts and models that focus specifically on change processes and how they can be executed most efficiently. Some changes are major initiatives that happen at a given point in time, such as a new building or a major new system, while others are smaller, such as improving operational processes. The evolutionary and ongoing nature of small change means that organizations are in a constant state of flux, and change, at the lower level at least, is an everyday occurrence. This means that it is important that people participate willingly and preferably enthusiastically in change, and are encouraged to do so by leaders who are aware of and respond to their need to adapt to change (as reflected in the coping cycle), and their legitimate reasons for resistance to change. Dunphy and Stace (1990) introduced the concept of change leadership, and suggested that different change leadership styles are appropriate in different change situations. Other authors have focused on the role of the change agent, the person who is a champion for change and drives change in organizations.

The final section in this chapter introduces the concept of innovation, arguing that the notion of 'change management' assumes a management imperative, and that innovation offers a potentially more creative perspective on moving things forward. Innovation can be considered at the organizational and individual levels. Ekvall made proposals for the nature of a creative organization climate, while, at the level of the individual, Pinchot introduced the concept of the intrapreneur, the enterprising and creative individual who works within a larger organization. A rather different perspective is to replace notions of change leadership with those of innovation leadership. There is considerable potential for further development of this perspective both in terms of theoretical models and practical experience.

Review questions

1 Make a list of the typical internal and external triggers of change experienced by organizations.

2 Discuss why change processes are complex and difficult to analyse, influence and manage.

3 What is the difference between initiative fatigue and initiative decay?

4 What is the Yerkes–Dodson hypothesis? Why is it relevant to change management?

5 Why do people resist change? What are Kotter and Schlesinger's recommended approaches for managing resistance to change?

6 What are Dunphy and Stace's four styles of leadership?

7 What are the required characteristics for a change agent?

8 Explain the ten dimensions of a creative organization climate. Why are these important?

9 Discuss the concepts 'sustaining innovations', 'disruptive innovation' and 'operational innovation'.

Challenges

1 How do managers identify a timeframe for a change process?

2 Is it possible to manage the interest of different stakeholder groups in a change process?

3 Is it possible to achieve a good balance of change relative to continuity?

4 How can one understand different individuals' responses to specific changes?

5 Can leaders adopt different change leadership styles to allow them to lead different kinds of change?

6 What is the relationship between change and innovation?

7 Can information organizations, often within the public sector, develop an organizational climate that will accommodate and encourage intrapreneurs?

Case study interview with Jane Hill, Wellington City Libraries, New Zealand

Jane Hill is Director, Wellington City Libraries Te Matapihi Ki Te Ao Nui, Wellington City Council, PO Box 1992, Wellington, New Zealand, and was co-leader of 'Public Libraries of New Zealand: a strategic framework 2006–2016'. A qualified librarian, Jane's main experience has been in the local government arena leading and managing different public library services. More recently she has combined managing the libraries with the Council's community services. (E-mail: jane.hill@wcc.govt.nz, see www.wcl.govt.nz)

Wellington City Libraries

The Wellington City Libraries network includes the central library and 11 branch libraries, specialist collections, the libraries' website and internet services, and a range of outreach programmes including books to babies and services to schools and the housebound. It has a staff of 151 FTEs (230 people). The city has a population of 184,000. Use of the libraries is very high with 77% of Wellingtonians registered as members. They borrow, on average, 19 items per person per year.

1   Can you list the major change projects or processes with which you have been involved over the past year?

At Wellington City Libraries change is part of the fabric of everyday life. I can refer to the major service reviews such as a different branch service model, which was developed as we are required to do on a triennial basis as part of the NZ Local Government Act. Another recent example would be the removal of our Mobile Library service. However, I think we get more change traction and business development from the plethora of smaller tactical change projects. While we often classify these at the level of product investigations, the combined effect in terms of our organization development and change is substantial. Almost all would involve changes in work flows, and impact on more than one library team's work, so change management processes are inbuilt into our daily thinking.

2 Which factors (internal and external) do you think have been the most important trigger for change for information services in the last five years?

I would summarize these as:

- ubiquity of online publishing and access so customers expect currency and access 24/7
- 'self-publishing' by customers and other interactive social networking trends
- Google and other 'first of mind' search engines for customers
- constancy of change.

These are general factors. I think closer to home there has been the willingness of our National Library of New Zealand to engage in collaborative service leadership. Several national information projects such as AnyQuestions (an online reference chat service staffed by major libraries) have resulted, as well as the shared development of pivotal documents such as the *National Digital Content Strategy* and *Strategic Framework for Public Libraries*. They have also provided leadership in achieving national funding for infrastructural development, which has been a prerequisite for regional information service change to occur.

3 In respect of continuity, can you identify five key things that have not changed in your information service over the past five years?

I would identify these as follows:

- The essence of our role in creating a variety of pathways to the world's best information, to match a variety of customer needs, has not changed.
- Customers have not changed the trend of their physical library usage, which has only continued to increase. However, they are making different selections on what they choose to visit for and ask about.
- Customer satisfaction with staff professionalism, and friendliness has each remained at 99–100% (independently measured annually by Nielsen).
- Customers' need 'to find out'. The more avenues we provide for access and self-service, and seek to raise the profile of what is on offer, the greater the customer thirst for 'more'.

- Our own need to balance the demands of the sexy 'early adopter' initiatives with existing services. These may be regarded as pedestrian and not worthy of comment, e.g. large print information services, but may be quietly used by many more customers than the new initiative.

4 Do you have a preference for evolutionary (tinkering) or transformational (kludging) change?

Not really. We have used both, and would want to use the best strategy to effect the desired result and employ a full range of organizational factors to achieve that end. This may include organizational structure, policies, strategy, employee agreements, funding, culture, etc. When I think back over my time as manager, within a business, at times we've been able to read the signs and anticipate. At others we've needed to be responsive and reactive to environmental factors. The aim is to be in step with our customers rather than driving them in any direction.

5 Have your proposals for change met with resistance? If so, what is your preferred approach to managing such resistance?

In a public service organization there will always be stakeholders who have a concern that we achieve the best outcome. That level of accountability is understood by my team and is not only to be expected, but welcomed as it sharpens our focus.

We aim first to be clear ourselves about the benefits and risks of any proposal, and that options have been investigated robustly. As the investigation proceeds, impact on a range of stakeholder groups will ideally form part of the consideration, e.g. how will it benefit a/b/c?

Where a significant niche impact is identified, and where practical, we begin involving them or their representatives in the development of the preferred option. For example, it may not be possible to include every individual but we would actively seek input from the Public Service (employee) Association throughout.

In addition, a detailed marketing and communications plan is developed. We often end up with several versions of the same proposal depending on the identified audience, where we would wish to tailor the benefits and rationale to the customer segment. Communicate often – it is impossible to over-communicate. For example during one large project, a weekly project newsbulletin called *Hill's hotlines* was established. This contained answers to questions as well as information about the project progress.

I also believe in offering customers and employees realistic choices. Not all things are possible, but it's a fact of life that adults will resist if they're presented with only one way forward.

We would also put transitional support in place. For example, during closure of the Mobile Library, each customer who solely used that library was personally contacted, and offered sessions with a buddy librarian who worked with them to achieve an equivalent level of library contact through a mix of other services we provide.

6   What are your particular strengths (and weaknesses?) as a change leader or change agent?

At times strengths and weaknesses can present similarly. The characteristics of my preferred approach are:

- working within a cross-functional team-based structure where accountability and engagement is shared; I think this is quite different from groups of people working together, and this has meant working with quite a variety of skills and competencies (not just librarianship and information technology) to be able to steer the organization towards such sustained customer endorsement; at times this can be time-consuming but I believe it has served us with better results
- sharing information frankly and openly and often
- being scrupulously fair about process in relation to staffing changes; trust is too precious an attribute to consider cutting corners here
- involving stakeholders in identifying the preferred solution; this is not just a risk mitigation strategy but essential to balancing (at times) conflicting needs within the context of a community-funded organization
- being willing to try different things (both in content and method), evaluate and move on
- ensuring ideas development and investment decisions are grounded in our investigation research for our own customer markets, not simply copied from what's working elsewhere.

References and additional reading

Abrahamson, E. (2000) Change Without Pain, *Harvard Business Review*, **78** (4), 75–9.

Advanced Institute of Management Research (2005) *Leadership for Innovation*, AIMR.

Brindley, L. (2007) A World Class Institution for the 21st Century, *Library and Information Update*, **6** (6), 19–21.

Christensen, C. M. and Overdorf, M. (2000) Meeting the Challenge of Disruptive Change, *Harvard Business Review*, **78** (2), 67–76.

Cunningham, I. (2005) Influencing People's Attitude to Change, *Professional Manager*, **14** (3), 37.

Dawson, P. (2003) *Understanding Organizational Change: the contemporary experience of people at work*, London, Sage.

Dunphy, D. C. and Stace, D. A. (1990) *Under New Management: Australian organizations in transition*, Sydney, McGraw-Hill.

Ekvall, G. (1996) Organizational Climate for Creativity and Innovation, *European Journal of Work and Organizational Psychology*, **5** (1), 105–23.

Ekvall, G. and Ryhammer, L. (1999) The Creative Climate: its determinants and effects at a Swedish university, *Creativity Research Journal*, **12** (4), 303–10.

Huczynski, A. A. and Buchanan, D. A. (2007) *Organizational Behaviour*, 6th edn, Harlow, Prentice Hall.

Kanter, R. M. (1989) *When Giants Learn to Dance: mastering the challenge of strategy, management and careers in the 1990s*, London, Simon and Schuster.

Kotter, J. P. (1995) Leading Change: why transformation efforts fail, *Harvard Business Review*, **73** (2), 12–20.

Kotter, J. P. (1999) *What Leaders Really Do*, Boston, MA, Harvard Business School Press.

Kotter, J. P. and Cohen, D. S. (2002) *The Heart of Change: real-life stories of how people change their organisations*, Boston, MA, Harvard Business School Press.

Kotter, J. P. and Schlesinger, L. A. (1979) Choosing Strategies for Change, *Harvard Business Review*, **57** (2), 106–14.

Kubler-Ross, E. (1969) *On Death and Dying*, Toronto, Macmillan.

Kuchi, T. (2006) Constant Change and the Strategic Role of Communication, *Library Management*, **27** (4/5), 218–35.

Levy, P. and Roberts, S. (2005) *Developing the New Learning Environment:*

the changing role of the academic librarian, London, Facet Publishing.

Lewin, K. (1951) *Field Theory in Social Science*, New York, Harper & Row.

Lougee, W. P. (2002) *Diffuse Libraries: emergent roles for the research library in the digital age*, Washington, DC, Council on Library and Information Resources.

Miller, D. (2004) Building Sustainable Change Capability, *Industrial and Commercial Training*, **36** (1), 9–12.

Mullins, L. J. (2007) *Management and Organizational Behaviour*, 8th edn, Harlow, FT Prentice Hall.

Mutula, S. M. (2000) Managing Stakeholder Interests During Change: the United States International University Library, Kenya, *Information Development*, **16** (2), 83–8.

Naylor, J. (2004) *Management*, 2nd edn, Harlow, FT Prentice Hall.

Neal, J. G. (2001) The Entrepreneurial Imperative: advancing from incremental to radical change in the academic library, *Portal: Libraries and the Academy*, **1** (91), 12–16.

Pettigrew, A. M. (1985) *The Awakening Giant: continuity and change in ICI*, Oxford, Blackwell.

Pettigrew, A. M. (ed.) (1987) *The Management of Strategic Change*, Oxford, Blackwell.

Pettinger, R. (2007) *Introduction to Management*, 4th edn, Basingstoke, Palgrave Macmillan.

Pinchot, G. (1984) *Intrapreneuring*, Thousand Oaks, CA, Sage.

Pors, N. O. (2003) Perspectives on Managing Change in Danish Libraries, *Journal of Academic Librarianship*, **29** (6), 411–15.

Riggs, D. E. (1989) Creativity, Innovation and Entrepreneurship in Libraries, Binghamton, NY, Haworth Press; also: *Journal of Library Administration*, **10** (2/3).

Riggs, D. E. (2001) The Crisis and Opportunities in Library Leadership, *Journal of Library Administration*, **32** (3/4), 5–17.

Siddiqui, M. A. (2003) Management for Change in Acquisitions in Academic Libraries, *The Electronic Library*, **21** (4), 352–7.

Smith, I. (2005) Managing the 'People' Side of Organizational Change, *Library Management*, **26** (3), 152–5.

Smith, I. (2006) Achieving Successful Organisational Change – do's and don'ts of change management, *Library Management*, **27** (4/5), 300–6.

Spies, P. B. (2000) Libraries, Leadership, and the Future, *Library Management*, **21** (3), 123–7.

Stace, D. and Dunphy, D. (2001) *Beyond the Boundaries: leading and re-creating the successful enterprise*, Sydney, McGraw-Hill.

Stephens, D. and Russell, K. (2004) Organizational Development, Leadership, Change, and the Future of Libraries, *Organizational Development and Leadership*, **53** (1), 1–4.

Toffler, A. (1970) *Future Shock*, London, Pan Books.

Winston, M. D. (2005) Library Leadership in Times of Crisis and Change, *New Library World*, **106** (9/10), 395–415.

Yerkes, R. M. and Dodson, J. D. (1908) The Relationship Strength of Stimulus to Rapidity of Habit-formation, *Journal of Comparative Neurology and Psychology*, **18**, 459–82.

5

Leading people

Learning objectives

After reading this chapter you should be able to:

☑ appreciate the complexity and challenges associated with leading people
☑ understand the importance of relationship building and the key steps associated with its success
☑ understand the concepts associated with empathy and emotional intelligence
☑ begin to consider approaches to leading individuals within a library and information context
☑ consider the impact of the individual leader on the motivation and morale of their staff
☑ understand the concept of empowerment and its role in leadership
☑ consider the importance of creating and developing teams
☑ understand the relevance of the concepts of followership and servantship.

Introduction

This chapter aims to explore the diverse and complex topic of leading people

– arguably the most challenging and most fundamental aspect of leadership. It can be argued that all of this book is concerned with leading people but this chapter addresses the issue directly. It begins with a discussion around the central notion of relationship building in a professional context, exploring trust and credibility and their connection with 'authentic' leadership. The chapter goes on to explore in detail approaches to leading individuals, including emotional intelligence, empathy, communication, empowerment and feedback. Particular attention is paid to motivation and morale and to tools and approaches such as coaching, mentoring and facilitation. The creation and development of teams is the focus of the next section, which explores several key team leadership concepts in detail. The next section considers notions of followership and servantship. The chapter concludes by raising the notion of hope, suggesting that the primary role of leaders is to foster hope within organizations. Throughout the chapter examples are provided that illustrate the application of concepts to the library and information context. Undoubtedly the challenge of leading others is one that keeps most leaders awake at night and raises the most difficulties; yet it also brings the most rewards as leaders see individuals develop, grow in their roles and shape their information service.

The challenge of leading people

The leadership of people is the leadership of complex and diverse individuals; it is frustrating, difficult, infuriating, inspiring, fulfilling and deeply motivating. Brockmeyer intimates that it is this aspect of leadership that is the 'soul' of library leadership. In her view 'leaders at their best touch the lives of the individuals with whom they work' (2005, 51). This is not necessarily easy or without conflict as leaders show us 'we can live expanded versions of ourselves' (2005, 52).

Bennis and Nanus (1997) outline four competencies that in their view will determine the success of new leadership in the 21st century; all four are intrinsically linked to leading people:

1   The new leader understands and practises the power of appreciation.
2   The new leader keeps reminding people of what is important.

3 The new leader sustains and generates trust.
4 The new leader and the led are intimate allies.

Consequently, as professionals in library and information services we must all recognize the centrality of leading people. How then do we do this to the best of our ability and with the best results? Our first step is relationship building.

REFLECTION Can you identify a leader in your life who has encouraged you to achieve? How did they do this?

Relationship building

As highlighted in Chapter 1, what 'followers' want from their leaders can be summarized as: *significance* (to feel valued), *community* (to feel part of something) and *excitement* (to feel challenged). Leadership is ultimately very personal and is based on relationships between people. Consequently, we emphasized in Chapter 1 that effective leaders are involved in connecting with people and building successful relationships. As many theorists argue, leadership is a relationship and any discussion of leadership must attend to the dynamics of this relationship. Working with others and building strong relationships is also one quarter of the Roberts and Rowley Leadership Diamond (Figure 1.2, page 16). So, although it is evident that relationship building is fundamental for leadership, it is far harder to pinpoint exactly how to do it! A key thing to remember is that leadership is not about the organization, the community, or the library service, it's about *you*.

What actions on behalf of the leader create, sustain and develop relationships? What actions can destroy them? Kouzes and Posner (2003) stress the importance of credibility. They researched on a wide and diverse scale what people want in leaders and received the same answer – people want leaders who are honest, forward-looking, competent and inspiring; they believe that this adds up to *credibility*. Credibility, they argue, is based on reputation, which develops over time and does not come automatically with a job or a title. It is also tightly interlinked with trust. Credibility can thus be gained in any role and at any level.

What positive actions can individuals undertake in order to develop their reputation and ultimately their credibility? Considering key leadership theorists, we would summarize positive actions to develop credibility in the following ways:

1 *Be a part of what is going on* – all too easily leaders can be isolated, separate from their colleagues and the actual work of the organization. As highlighted in Chapter 2, there has been a shift from notions of hierarchy and control to notions of community and engagement. Employees are no longer considered as 'subordinates' and leaders should make concerted efforts to get to know their colleagues at all levels.

2 *Be visible* – people need to know you on a personal level in order to trust you. Leaders must interact with people regularly and not just formally through meetings but informally. Leaders must be accessible and 'out there' in the library and information service and the wider organization.

3 *Be honest and open* – people respect honesty even if it is bad news. Being open will help to create transparency and an environment where individuals know where they stand.

4 *Be personable* – be prepared to give of yourself: 'By sharing personal experiences, telling their stories, and joining in, leaders become people, not just holders of positions.' (Kouzes and Posner, 2003, 46) Relationships should involve the whole person and not separate work from home life.

5 *Be a good listener* – this is covered later in this chapter and is absolutely critical to relationship building.

6 *Become an employee for the day* – many organizations have introduced the concept of 'Back to the Floor', which aims to put leaders back on the frontline, reminding them of the work that their staff do but also providing an insight into problems that they may then be able to resolve.

The negative actions that undermine and harm relationship building can be summarized as the reverse of the above – by being remote, insulated and depersonalized (particularly through technology such as e-mail) people won't know their leaders, there is no connection and no relationship, and consequently no credibility and trust.

REFLECTION Consider the positive actions listed above that are needed to build personal credibility. How easy do you think it would be to do all of these regularly?

The impact of a leader who has credibility is evident from Kouzes and Posner's research. They found that when people perceive their managers to have high credibility they are far more likely to:

◆ be proud to tell others they are part of the organization
◆ feel a strong sense of team spirit
◆ see their own personal values as consistent with those of the organization
◆ feel attached and committed to the organization
◆ have a sense of ownership for the organization.

There are also several questions that leaders can ask themselves to assess their own trustworthiness. Reflect on the following and consider where you could make improvements to enhance your personable credibility with others:

1 Is my behaviour predictable or erratic?
2 Do I communicate clearly or carelessly?
3 Do I treat promises seriously or lightly?
4 Am I forthright or dishonest?

Relationship building is thus based on credibility and trust. As the key elements explored above indicate, this is predicated on not only self-awareness but a willingness to share that self openly with others.

Understanding and leading individuals

In order to lead others, at whatever level and in whatever role, we must fully attempt to understand them as individuals. Yet understanding individuals' needs and values is made more difficult in today's complex work environments and in a context when everyone is pressed for time. We must also appreciate the diversity of people, their world views and experiences which can be so different from our own.

One way of enhancing mutual understanding is to solicit and give feedback regularly. An effective leader learns the art of feedback and recognizes its importance given the different perspectives and interpretations individuals can have of messages and situations. They also seek out feedback on their own behaviour, performance and impact on others regularly. There are different models for this which can be adapted according to circumstances. These include:

◆ performance appraisal
◆ 360 degree performance appraisals (to gain feedback from peers, your manager, your own staff)
◆ feedback to an individual on their progress that is constructive and highlights positives as well as areas to build on
◆ asking for feedback in terms of your management and leadership – feedback is most effective when it is focused on a specific aspect of your work, is honest, is openly received and can be applied.

Adair (Thomas, 2004) believes that feedback is not given at all or not often enough in organizations, usually for the following reasons:

1   People don't need to be told how they are doing, they already know.
2   People take it easy if you say things are going well.
3   They are unhappy and cause trouble if you say things are not going well.
4   We lack the skills or time to do it.

Certainly the last of these points is an issue and leaders should dedicate time to developing their skills in this area. Feedback which is affirmative must be accurate, sincere, generous, fair and must not be patronizing, condescending or calculated for effect. A useful framework for giving constructive feedback when you wish someone's behaviour to change is Beatty and McGill's (1995, 159):

1   Clarity – Be clear about what you want to say.
2   Emphasize the positive – This isn't being collusive in the person's dilemma.
3   Be specific – Avoid general comments and clarify pronouns such as 'it', 'that', etc.

4 Focus on behaviour rather than the person.

5 Refer to behaviour that can be changed.

6 Be descriptive rather than evaluative.

7 Own the feedback – Use 'I' statements.

8 Generalizations – Notice 'all', 'never', 'always' etc., and ask to get more specificity – often these words are arbitrary limits on behaviour.

9 Be very careful with advice – People rarely struggle with an issue because of the lack of some specific piece of information; often, the best help is helping the person to come to a better understanding of their issue, how it developed, and how they can identify actions to address the issue more effectively.

We would also add, be persistent, don't expect people to change overnight, but be prepared to keep addressing issues and providing feedback.

REFLECTION Apply the model above to a specific scenario where you need to give feedback to someone in your life either at home or at work.

Examples of giving and generating feedback in a library service context can be found in Table 5.1.

Table 5.1 Examples of feedback from library service contexts

Context	Example of feedback	Impact
A team member in a library management team has become increasingly reserved in meetings.	The team leader meets the team member on a 1–1 basis and describes the behaviour that has been noticed. They ask what is wrong, demonstrating concern for the individual but also highlighting what behaviour they expect in meetings from members of the team.	The team member acknowledges they have problems at home that are preoccupying them at work and making them feel more isolated. They talk about what support they need and what is expected and agree a way forward that they will monitor.
A library assistant has worked hard on a new publicity campaign within a public library that has been a great success.	Their manager feeds back to the assistant how much they appreciate their work and encourages them to submit an application for a national award for innovation in libraries.	The library assistant feels extremely motivated and decides to develop their skills in this area, as well as applying for the award.

Listening is also an integral aspect of understanding others. The concepts of active listening and reflective listening are particularly useful in this context. Adair (Thomas, 2004) sees listening skills as centring on five attributes:

◆ being willing to listen
◆ clearly hearing the message
◆ interpreting the meaning (the speaker's meaning, not only your interpretation)
◆ evaluating carefully (suspending judgement at first but then assessing value and usefulness)
◆ responding appropriately – remembering communication is a two-way street.

As highlighted in Chapter 2, Goleman's work on the concept of emotional intelligence (1996) can be viewed as the most important step forward in understanding our own emotions, the emotions of others and their impact on relationships. An overview of EI as a concept and in relation to knowing yourself as a leader is included in Chapter 2. In considering leading others, and getting the best out of individuals, think through the exercises in Figure 5.1, which highlight the benefits of developing your emotional intelligence in both a personal and professional capacity.

Motivation and morale

Leaders at all levels of library and information services must consider the motivation of staff and colleagues a key priority. In order to influence motivation we must first understand motivational theory and the individuals we are working with – as highlighted above. People behave differently – their motivation and morale can ebb and flow – as the result of a wide range of very complex factors, from personality to experiences, values and organizational culture. Two different views of motivation are those of Maslow and Herzberg. Maslow's (1954) Hierarchy of Needs has been extremely influential in developing understanding of behaviour dependent on a range of motives. This is represented in Figure 5.2. The basic levels must be satisfied if individuals are to progress to the higher levels; however, it must not be assumed that

The shouting match: A discussion between you and your partner has escalated into a shouting match. You are both upset and in the heat of the argument start making personal attacks which neither of you really mean. What is the best thing to do?

[A] Agree to take a 20-minute break before continuing the discussion.
[B] Go silent, regardless of what your partner says.
[C] Say you are sorry, and ask your partner to apologize too.
[D] Stop for a moment, collect your thoughts, then restate your side of the case as precisely as possible.

The most emotionally intelligent answer is A. In these circumstances, the most appropriate behaviour is to take a 20-minute break. As the argument has intensified, so have the physiological responses in your nervous system, to the point at which it will take at least 20 minutes to clear your body of these emotions of anger and arousal. Any other course of action is likely merely to aggravate an already tense and uncontrolled situation.

The uninspired team: You have been given the task of managing a team that has been unable to come up with a creative solution to a work problem. What is the first thing that you do?

[A] Draw up an agenda, call a meeting and allot a specific period of time to discuss each item.
[B] Organize an off-site meeting aimed specifically at encouraging the team to get to know each other better.
[C] Begin by asking each person individually for ideas about how to solve the problem.
[D] Start out with a brainstorming session, encouraging each person to say whatever comes to mind, no matter how wild.

The most emotionally intelligent answer is B. As a leader of a group of individuals charged with developing a creative solution, your success will depend on the climate that you can create in your project team. Creativity is likely to be stifled by structure and formality; instead, creative groups perform at their peaks when rapport, harmony and comfort levels are most high. In these circumstances, people are most likely to make the most positive contributions to the success of the project.

The indecisive young manager: You have recently been assigned a young manager in your team, and have noticed that he appears to be unable to make the simplest of decisions without seeking advice from you. What do you do?

[A] Accept that he 'does not have what it take to succeed around here' and find others in your team to take on his tasks.
[B] Get an HR manager to talk to him about where he sees his future in the organization.
[C] Purposely give him lots of complex decisions to make so that he will become more confident in the role.
[D] Engineer an ongoing series of challenging but manageable experiences for him, and make yourself available to act as his mentor.

The most emotionally intelligent answer is D. Managing others requires high levels of emotional intelligence, particularly if you are going to be successful in maximizing the performance of your team. Often, this means that you need to tailor your approach to meets the specific needs of the individual, and provide them with support and feedback to help them grow in confidence and capability.

Figure 5.1 Some examples of exercises in emotional intelligence (extracted from http://ei.haygroup.com)

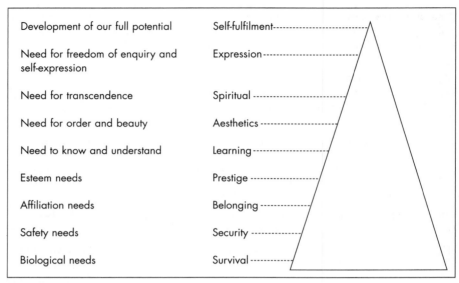

Figure 5.2 Maslow's Hierarchy of Needs

everyone needs all levels, nor that they seek satisfaction on all levels from the workplace, as other activities and interests and relationships can act as satisfiers. Herzberg's (1966) work is based on a similar premise but suggests we must improve the factors classified as 'dissatisfiers' while also increasing the level of 'satisfiers' as represented in Table 5.2.

Table 5.2 Herzberg's satisfiers and dissatisfiers

Satisfiers	**Dissatisfiers**
Motivators	Hygiene factors (must be provided to avoid dissatisfaction)
Achievement	Salary
Recognition from others	Job security
Responsibility	Working conditions
Opportunities for advancement	Status
Interpersonal relationships	Fringe benefits
The work itself	Company policy and administration

REFLECTION How would you assess you own current motivational state? Which of Herzberg's motivators might help you to increase your sense of motivation?

Considering these views, how can a leader attempt to motivate their staff? The individual themselves obviously has a key role to play in their own motivation – and a leader's role can be to highlight this to individual members of staff who expect other people to solve all their problems. A leader must also attempt to really understand an individual's state of motivation and consider ways in which they can both provide the 'hygiene factors' required such as job security and good working conditions, and also increased 'satisfiers' such as celebrating achievements and providing opportunities for enhancement via professional development. Adair (Thomas, 2004) also suggests six principles for leaders to embed in their working lives to aid motivation:

1   Be motivated yourself.
2   Select people who are highly motivated.
3   Set realistic and challenging targets.
4   Remember that progress motivates.
5   Provide fair rewards.
6   Give recognition.

There are times, however, when we will be faced with the challenge of motivating individuals who are viewed as 'problem people'. They often appear entrenched in their views, can be negative, and have no enthusiasm for their role or organization. Nicholson (2003) and Taylor (2002) suggest an alternative approach to this challenge than simply trying to influence the individual to take your view point. They advocate building rapport by thinking differently, by listening (really listening), identifying what the individual's greatest need is, by offering to help them with that and by following it through. Kouzes and Posner (2003) also suggest that leaders must not only motivate, they must *inspire*. They identify five characteristics of exemplary leaders who do inspire; in Table 5.3 we present these characteristics and provide examples from library and information contexts.

Table 5.3 Inspiring leaders

Characteristic of exemplary leader	Information services example
Leaders challenge the process. They experiment and take risks, constantly challenging other people to exceed their own limitations.	A learning advisor in an academic library explores the use of new technologies to delivery information literacy sessions; they influence their colleagues and academic staff to pilot the approach and evaluate.
Leaders inspire a shared vision. They envision an enabling future and enlist people to join in that new direction.	A newly appointed special library manager revitalizes their team by opening up discussions about the future of the service, which has lost its sparkle and has a low profile in the organization.
Leaders enable others to act. They strengthen others and foster collaboration.	A library director empowers their team to make service improvements by listening, providing the resources and the encouragement.
Leaders model the way. They set the example for people by their own leadership behaviour and they plan small wins to get the process moving.	A public library team leader remains cheerful and positive in light of uncertainty with structural changes and focuses on providing staff with as much information as possible.
Leaders encourage the heart. They regard and recognize individual contributions and they celebrate success.	Staff from across a large and complex library organization organize a mid-year celebration to recognize the work that has been completed so far that year.

Coaching, mentoring and facilitating

The concepts of coaching, mentoring and facilitation are additional valuable tools for leading individuals. They are covered in more detail in Chapter 7, 'Leadership Development', but will be introduced briefly here. They each have significant benefits for the individual, the organization and the leader who can extend their skills in getting the best out of people. These three concepts are also closely aligned with the notion of transformational and participatory leadership that moves beyond 'command and control'. They can be described in the following ways:

1   *Coaching* is a one-to-one approach aiming to develop specific skills in an individual or to enhance performance in some way. Coaching is specific in focus and therefore quite different from (although often confused with) mentoring. Coaching could be used where an individual has taken

on new responsibilities and is struggling with one element, for example project management or managing staff for the first time.

2   *Mentoring* is a one-to-one holistic approach to professional and personal development, which can be formal or informal; mentoring involves considering the 'whole person', their career, their skills and what they need in order to succeed. Mentoring is particularly valid for individuals in new roles or who are at key stages in their careers. Mentoring could be used where an individual is at a crossroads in their career, for example a branch library manager who has returned from a career break while having a family and is feeling unconfident and unsure of the future.

3   *Facilitation* can be used as a one-to-one technique or for a group. Facilitation skills are extremely valuable to leaders as facilitation literally means to 'make things easy' and aims to bring out the best in people both in an individual and team context. Typical facilitation events include meetings, brainstorming future scenarios for the service and alleviating and resolving conflict within a team.

In all three concepts, the skills of active listening and rapport building, as previously discussed, are crucial. In leading individuals, we must recognize that relationship building is the first and most vital step. Without this, other concepts such as motivation or coaching are meaningless.

REFLECTION Have you ever experienced mentoring or coaching? What was the impact on you? If you haven't experienced them, what benefits do you think they could bring?

Before leaving this section on understanding and leading individuals, let us consider the concept of *empowerment*. Leaders 'empower others to translate intention into reality and to sustain it' (Bennis and Nanus, 1997, 74). Empowerment requires the clarification of authority and boundaries so that individuals at all levels understand the scope of their own power and the decisions they can make. Empowerment requires the engagement of individuals and can also increase engagement if individuals feel that they have clear authority and are directly responsible for their own work and for making a difference. Rather than empowerment being seen as a distinct and separate activity that leaders do – 'I am now going to empower you in your role' – we would argue that empowerment should be integrated into relationship development at all stages.

In a library and information context, empowerment can and should occur at all levels and can be facilitated by:

◆ an open and honest information-sharing culture
◆ management that trusts their employees
◆ employees who give their full commitment
◆ organizational culture that allows people to make mistakes
◆ managers who assume the role of coach and mentor to help their team and individuals achieve the desired results
◆ established parameters
◆ employees who understand and internalize the corporate strategic objectives.

One example of effective empowerment within a library and information context is front-line public service staff feeling able and confident to make decisions to ensure customer satisfaction rather than constantly having to refer customers with questions or problems to managers.

Creating and leading teams

In considering leadership functions with regard to teams, all of the issues explored above in relation to leading individuals apply. We must in addition consider team development theories, particularly as so many library and information services are introducing increasingly team-based structures to address the challenges facing them. As Handy (1993) highlights, individuals spend so much of their working lives in groups – whether formally or informally – that if leaders have a good understanding of how groups and teams are formed, interact and work, they can better approach the task of developing 'high-performance teams'. We must also ask ourselves why teams are so important and so prevalent throughout society. Sir Alex Ferguson's words convey the power of the team as more than a collective of individuals, and more important than strategy: 'Tactics are important but they do not win football matches. Players win football matches. The best teams stand out because they are teams, because the individual players have been truly integrated so that the team functions with a single spirit' (in Kermally, 2004, 75).

One of the most important tasks a leader will ever do is to create and develop their team – whether this be for a specific project, for service operations or for senior management and leadership. A useful model to further our understanding of teams is Tuckman and Jensen's (1977) theory of group formation, represented in Figure 5.3. They identify five stages of development, from forming through to mourning, when a group concludes its business and is disbanded or moves on. Leaders within information services need to be aware and recognize each stage, knowing how to support each phase successfully. The stages of group formation are described below:

1   During *forming* the group is under-developed and is just beginning to organize itself to achieve common goals, but there can be a high level of anxiety and uncertainty causing tensions within the group. The role of the team leader in this stage is to establish goals and direction.

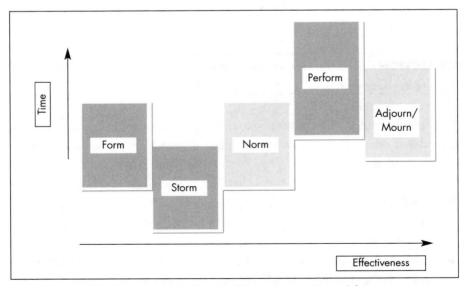

Figure 5.3 The five stages of group formation (adapted from Tuckman and Jensen, 1977)

2   During *storming* the group is experimenting, gaining confidence, exploring issues. Conflict may emerge as may rebellion against the leader. The team leader's role in this stage is to resolve tensions and this can be done by establishing trust and facilitating open discussions.

3   During *norming* consolidation occurs, problems are resolved, and there is mutual support and group cohesion, personal relationships and interaction, clarification of task and agreement of objectives. The leader's role here is to continue to build rapport and provide a conducive environment for the team.

4   During *performing* we see achievement of the team, openness, flexibility, co-operation and cohesion. The team may reach the level of being a 'high performing' team.

5   Performance may naturally lead to *adjourning* or mourning as the task is completed or members of the group move on. The role of the leader at this stage is to facilitate reflection, reassure and ensure that the group moves back to forming if it is to continue (perhaps with new members). It should be stressed that every time a group's membership alters it must reassess its position as it will begin again at the forming stage. Groups can also get 'stuck' at different stages and a team leader must be able to recognize this and formulate what needs to happen to move the team on.

REFLECTION Consider a team you are a member of. How would you describe its stage of development?

Multiple variables can impact on a team's effectiveness and must be considered when creating and developing a team. These variables can be summarized as:

◆   *establishing the purpose of the team* – maximize a team's performance by having a clear definition and understanding of the task, plus defining and allocating workloads and authority

◆   *establishing team cohesion* – via the clear development and articulation and agreement of norms, behaviours, values, size of the team, communication channels and approaches

◆ *establishing effective group structures* – this relates to group dynamics and how each individual relates to the others
◆ *establishing the team members and balanced team roles* – ensure the right blend of skills and competencies for the task (for example someone who is a financial expert will be vital for a team who are managing a large building redevelopment) but also the right balance of team role types; there are multiple theories of team types with Belbin's (1981) team role theory and model, which is still extremely popular and widely used; his nine team types are seen as vital for a high performing team (see Figure 5.4) with the team leader's role being to assess the team members (via a self-assessment questionnaire) and also to develop them where necessary; there is a distinction between team roles and functional roles and individuals can have strong preferences for several team types; it should be emphasized that Belbin's model has been criticized for being overtly psychological and simplistic
◆ *establishing learning* – ensure continuous learning through reflection, development and training, and the establishment of a culture that fosters learning at all levels.

Chairman/Co-ordinator – organizer, disciplined, strong sense of objectives, good at working with others
Plant or innovator – ideas person, creative input, source of ideas and knowledge
Resource investigator – explores ideas and resources outside the group, has good networks and draws on these
Shaper – task focused, will push decisions forward and look for the best course of action
Monitor-evaluator – analyses suggestions and evaluates their feasibility and practical value
Team worker – focuses on the needs of the group, will be supportive and diplomatic
Implementer – a practical organizer, will transform ideas into practical steps
Completer – attention to detail, will follow things through and be conscientious
Specialist – brings a specialist expertise, skills or knowledge as required

---

Figure 5.4 Belbin's nine team roles

But what about when leaders inherit a team? what if the team is dysfunctional or not performing as required? There are several options:

1   Assess why the team are not working well – consider issues around cohesion and the balance of team members and roles.

2   Assess your own role and what else you need to do.
3   Consider team-building activities to enable the team to get to know and trust each other.
4   Consider changing the team dynamics by introducing a new team member who has a particularly needed attitude or skills set.
5   Consider changing the team dynamics by removing a member of the team (if they are particularly disruptive).
6   Consider reviewing with the team their terms of reference to ensure clarity of purpose, their values and their goals.

A refreshing antidote to theories of team development (which can appear to some as too formulaic and mechanistic) such as Belbin's comes from Taylor (2002) who tells us to 'Forget Belbin and the other team-working fads and theories; it is when people work hard for each other that true, total and long-term teamwork is achieved' (105). Taylor goes on to suggest that a leader's role is to create alignment and integration between the individual, their needs and goals, and those of the organization. In order to do this, leaders must build a culture that values all individuals; they can do this by:

◆   encouraging open and blame-free debate within your team; drawing out everyone's contributions, hopes, fears and ideas for the future
◆   being a visible leader, talking and listening to people
◆   consulting widely and putting in place a set of values that everyone can identify with
◆   catching people doing something right and openly praising them.

One of the most influential theories of team leadership is the 'task – team – individual' model developed by John Adair (Thomas, 2004). Adair sees the leadership functions required by a team as three overlapping needs as depicted in Figure 5.5. These three needs are explained as:

◆   *task needs* – to achieve the common need/purpose/goal
◆   *team maintenance needs* – to be held together or to maintain themselves as a team
◆   *individual needs* – the needs which individuals bring to the group.

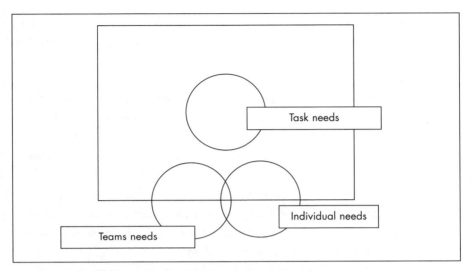

Figure 5.5 Task, teams and individual needs (Adair)

A leader has a function in each need as they are expected to help the team achieve the common *task*, build the synergy of *teamwork*, and respond to *individuals* and meet their needs. The three needs are represented as overlapping because they each contribute to the other two in different ways; for example, by achieving the task we build the team and satisfy the individual. Conversely, failure to assure one element will affect the others; for example, if team maintenance fails, performance on that task will be impaired and individual satisfaction reduced.

Applying this model to the library and information services context demonstrates how effective it can be if leaders consider each need and develop qualities to ensure the needs are met. The case study below illustrates one such example from a national library perspective.

Case study: meeting the needs of task, team and individual in a national library context

Background

The senior team in the national library have a major challenge ahead of them with the need to develop new models for service delivery that encompass increased digital delivery and heighten standards. The team leader provides leadership across Adair's three needs in the following ways but leadership is also provided by others within the team for each element.

- *Task*: the leader initiates the discussion to get the group moving and to stress the importance of developing new models in the context of decreasing usage and budgetary problems. The leader defines the task clearly and is honest in establishing the facts of the situation, ensuring efficiency and perseverance when the task looks too difficult.
- *Team*: the leader creates trust within the team through their own integrity, and relieves tension through humour and by maintaining a sense of proportion. They demonstrate honesty and humility and ensure that each member of the team feels they are playing a full part in the decision-making.
- *Individual*: the leader demonstrates tact in dealing with each person; they are compassionate when discussing issues that directly affect one member of the team. They are consistent and just and this 'fair dealing' encourages each person to raise suggestions as to the way forward.

The leader must therefore create the right atmosphere for the team to thrive and succeed. They promote teamwork and get to know, encourage and motivate each individual. Essentially leadership is a 'relationship through which one person influences the behaviour or actions of other people', therefore it cannot be separated from the activities of groups and effective teambuilding (Mullins, 2005).

The facilitation of teams requires particular skills encompassing a high degree of group management and communication techniques. These can be summarized as:

- setting the scene and rapport building (with each individual and as a group)
- stimulating interest in the group for the topic (why is it so important?)
- valorizing every participant and their contributions
- seeking consensus – where everyone agrees to agree
- providing focus particularly with regard to priority items and areas for discussion

◆ recognizing common themes and trends and drawing these to the group's attention
◆ moving the group towards action with clear accountability.

Establishing a strong sense of purpose or mission, and creating and realizing vision will be explored in Chapter 6; in the context of leading teams the concept of developing a *shared vision* has been highlighted by many authors, including Bennis and Senge:

> A vision is truly shared when you and I have a similar picture and are committed to one another having it, not just to each of us, individually, having it. When people truly share a vision they are connected, bound together by a common aspiration. Personal visions derive their power from an individual's deep caring for the vision. Shared visions derive their power from a common caring. (Senge, 1990)

REFLECTION How can a leader facilitate the development of a shared vision?

As highlighted earlier, many library and information services are introducing increasingly team-based structures to address the challenges facing them. We must be aware of the wide range of types of teams that can be put in place and used for different purposes. Depending on the type of team, a leader may focus on different approaches; for example a cross-functional team that operates on a matrix management model will require significant clarity in terms of goals and roles, plus considerable rapport building between members who may experience tensions between competing responsibilities. A strategic team that focuses on future direction and decision making will require a strong shared vision and high levels of trust. Virtual teams have also developed within library and information services and can be particularly valuable for project teams who are distributed across a geographical area; a leader in this context will focus on communication to build rapport and to clarify goals.

Followership and servantship

There has been increasing interest in the concept of 'followership' which envisages leadership as part of a dynamic relationship. As Goffee and Jones (2006) state, 'Followers are the other side of the leadership equation. Without them there is no relationship and no leadership. If leadership is a dynamic relationship . . . it is logical that followers, too, live in the same dynamic relationship, but see things from a different perspective' (189).

If a leader considers all the elements we have explored within this chapter, and commits time and energy to knowing their followers and building relationships with them, then followers will feel 'comfortable' in themselves, in their relationship and in their role within the team and organization. It should also be stressed that everyone is a follower, and that there are times when leaders at all levels must be followers. We have reflected elsewhere in this book what followers expect from leaders and what qualities go towards effective leaderships but what makes a good follower? Evidence suggests that good followers:

◆ *are prepared to speak up* – to tell it like it is even if this is not what their leaders want to hear; they care about the organization, its mission and its success
◆ *are able to be themselves* and are aware of their own strengths and weaknesses and know what they do best
◆ *have a skilful appreciation of change and timing* and accept some degree of ambiguity and uncertainty; they don't expect their leaders to have all the answers and to solve all problems
◆ *are able to support the leader actively and compliment them*, but only when it is deserved and has been earned.

All leaders must consider their own followership qualities and know when to act as a follower. Good followers may also ultimately become leaders!

REFLECTION Considering the four characteristics of a good follower, how would you assess your own 'followership'? Are there areas you need to work on?

The notion of 'servantship' is closely aligned to that of 'stewardship' – the idea that a leader is responsible for the safeguarding and best interests of the organization and its staff. Brockmeyer (2005) chooses stewardship as one of the sought after leadership qualities, where leaders choose service (to the library service and to their team) over self-interest. This in many ways may seem obvious but examples of 'bad leadership' often expose individuals whose own self-interests and political ambitions are far more important than the development of their staff or the well-being of their service. In conclusion, 'Effective leaders deploy their differences to serve both their own and the team's interests. In effect, they convey the reassuring message that "if you fall, I will catch you" ' (Goffee and Jones, 2006, 48).

A leader's ultimate goal?

We have discussed throughout this chapter the importance of motivating individuals, building relationships, creating rapport, developing teams and sharing visions. All of these are challenging and require great skill, self-awareness and risk taking. This brings us to the final and most simple leadership concept of this chapter – *hope*. The fostering of hope within people and within organizations is viewed by many authors as the most important element when considering the leadership of people: 'Hope is a necessary element for leaders since it has implications for action – visioning, planning . . . and for interpersonal relatedness and community building' (Walker, 2006).

Hope builds confidence in the future and conveys that things can and will be better. As Kanter (2004) expresses it, 'We look to leaders for confidence . . . Leadership is not about the leader, it is about how he or she build the confidence of everyone else.' Kouzes and Posner (1999) describe how leaders generate and sustain the hope of those within their organizations when they 'set high standards and genuinely express optimism about an individual's capacity to achieve them', when they give internal support, when they coach others and when they set an example themselves. In the context of great change and uncertainty within library and information services, hope can be very powerful and can also be contagious.

Summary and conclusions

This chapter has aimed to engage with the complexities of leading people, emphasizing that in order to be successful leaders must genuinely engage with individuals; without this organizations are left with empty mission statements and a missed connection between people and purpose. Leaders at all levels can have a positive impact on individual motivation and achievement, and on team effectiveness and development. In order to do this they must be both self-aware and willing to give of themselves to build their credibility. This credibility is the foundation for the development of the skills and approaches we have explored here. Effective leaders focus on the task, individual and team to create an environment conducive with success; they take time to understand what motivates individuals and what they can do to enhance that motivation while also ensuring their own motivation remains high. Leaders must also develop their own 'followership' abilities as well as encouraging those abilities in others. In conclusion, we must remember and respect that we are working with people who demand and require a great deal of us but who also give a great deal in return: 'I, as a whole person, come into work each day, and they get all of me: my hopes, dreams, desires and problems, my passion and creativity as well as less favourable attributes such as my pride in my need for recognition and support' (Brockmeyer, 2005, 158).

Review questions

1 How would you define the concept of credibility? How can it be developed professionally?
2 What actions by leaders could undermine their credibility?
3 How can we ensure that the giving and receiving of feedback is a positive experience to those involved?
4 Discuss some of the theoretical models that leaders can use to help them to motivate others.
5 Define coaching, mentoring and facilitation – how can they be applied to an individual or group context?
6 Describe the different stages of group formation. What is the leader's role at each stage?
7 In terms of team leadership, why are tasks, teams and individuals inter-related?
8 Define followership. What makes a good follower?

Challenges

1   Is the challenge of leadership in library and information services really all about the challenge of leading people?
2   How can we be confident that we have credibility?
3   Why is giving feedback so important in leadership terms and why is it so difficult?
4   Why are different types of teams emerging within library organizations? How can they best be led?
5   Can personal and organizational visions be integrated or will there always be some degree of conflict?
6   How can we ensure that leaders are not primarily motivated by self-interest?

Case study interview with Leo Appleton, Learning Resources Manager, West Cheshire College, UK

Leo Appleton is the Learning Resources Manager at West Cheshire College, a large further education college in north west England. The department is a fully converged library, IT, e-learning and digital media support service, and is well embedded into the curriculum activity of the college. Leo's professional interests include integration of learning resource services into teaching and learning and in particular within e-learning activities and developments.

He has previously worked in a number of higher and further education colleges, where he has developed and led many electronic resources and e-learning initiatives and projects. He was part of the team awarded runner up in the 2003 *Times Higher Education Supplement* e-learning award. Leo has presented papers at many conferences on the topics of promoting e-resources, e-books, e-learning and information literacy and has published several articles on e-book developments and the embedding of electronic library resources into virtual learning environments.

1   Throughout your career how have you approached relationship building with colleagues? What have you found most successful?

Healthy professional relationships are fundamental to effective management and leadership. I cannot say that I have deliberately employed strategies in order to form particular relationships, but on reflection I suppose there are certain practices that I demonstrate, which allow for relationship building to take place. Relationships with individuals are formed through dialogue and two-way discussion, which should include effective and active listening, which I suppose are key to how I like to communicate with individual staff members.

Consistent communication is all important, along with being available and approachable to staff. Obviously, the larger the department, the more difficult it is to ensure that time is available for every individual member of staff, which is where effective line management needs to be deployed. It is important to hold regular one-to-one review meetings with those reporting to you directly, and in turn encourage this practice with the teams and individuals that they manage. This allows for regular and dedicated time to discuss individual working needs within a strategic and operational context. The benefit of this is that over a relatively short period of time you can get to know the individual strengths and weaknesses of your team. I then like to play to individuals' strengths, so that I know that they are working within some sort of a comfort zone, while also identifying particular areas for development. I have also found that it is important to allow individuals to complete particular tasks and operations with minimal interference from me, while still being available in a support capacity, especially if it is something that I am particularly interested in (i.e. letting go of things that you were once personally responsible for, and subsequently proud of).

More informal mechanisms include little things like taking time out for lunch and coffee breaks, and getting to know individuals through general conversation. Similarly, spending time with individual staff while they are on the shop floor or shadowing or assisting them in their routine operations is a highly effective way of building relationships. And although it can often appear that other tasks get sidelined, it is useful to regularly spend some time working directly with colleagues at service points or on projects.

2 How do you assess you own personal credibility? How important is that to you?

In the further education colleges I have worked in I have been responsible for managing changes within the Learning Resources departments. This whole process tests out how credibly you are perceived by your staff, especially when trying to implement change quickly. The changes that I have been responsible for implementing include introducing marketing and promotional concepts; creating and developing

Learning Resources web pages; establishing electronic resources and e-book collections; implementing a virtual learning environment; and the most challenging of all, converging library, IT and audiovisual services.

Creating and sustaining credibility among those staff who are in the middle of all this change is one of the most difficult aspects of the job, but is highly important with regard to how you are perceived as a leader. Similarly, your own morale and self-esteem can be affected if you do not maintain a level of credibility among the staff whose environment you are changing. As the leader of a department, I need to feel that I am perceived as confident and credible by my own managers, but most importantly of all by the customers of the service. Having the backing of curriculum areas within the college is a useful way of achieving this. You are then in a position to ensure that the changes you make are responsive and being driven by customer consultation.

Credibility is extremely important to me and it is important to demonstrate success in what you are trying to achieve. This can come through regular quality assurance mechanisms such as user surveys, staff surveys, student focus groups, performance indicators, etc. If you truly believe in the changes that you are making, then service improvements should follow, and with this should come the qualitative and anecdotal evidence which can be used to demonstrate success, and therefore also credibility.

Some staff will always resist change, and effective communication is essential within the change process. I always try to include all staff in discussion about change, so that decisions are democratically informed and the rationale behind them effectively explained.

3 What strategies do you use for communicating with your colleagues?

I try to use a variety of communication techniques in order to enter into dialogues and discussions, support colleagues, make decisions, and keep staff briefed and informed. My particular strategies include a meeting schedule, published in advance, so that those involved are aware of forthcoming discussion and have the opportunity to contribute to agendas and to attend:

- regular (weekly) individual meetings with my five team managers
- weekly senior team meetings with team managers
- monthly full departmental meetings (blend of operational and developmental discussion)

- termly e-learning development meetings (involving cross-college staff)
- termly digital media meetings
- regular team meetings and one-to-one review meetings between team managers and their team members.

Minutes and notes of all meetings are made available to all staff, as are the annual report, quality documentation, survey results and internal strategic documents.

In addition I communicate via a monthly update e-mail, in which I am able to brief all staff with college-wide information and employ an 'idea of the month' initiative to encourage team members to be innovative and to suggest useful changes.

On a wider level, colleagues outside the department (our customers) are communicated with through:

- regular attendance at curriculum planning meetings by Learning Resources liaison staff
- a regular Learning Resources newsletter distributed college wide.

4 Do you regularly give and request feedback? What impact do you feel this has on individuals and on your organization?

I continually seek customer feedback (user surveys, staff surveys, student focus groups). This provides a basis for discussion and ensures that the service is responsive and change is driven by the customer.

However, it is equally important to request feedback from my own staff. I often find conflicting views among staff, particularly those whose roles have changed through convergence of services, which is why I find it useful to have discussion based around customer feedback.

I also find that large meetings are not the most practical method for getting staff to feed back their thoughts and opinions about changes, issues and developments. Staff tend to work well and feel less inhibited in smaller groups, so I often allow time during our full staff meetings for small group discussions to be fed back to the wider group. I think that this particular mechanism enables staff to feel valued and listened to, as well as providing an opportunity for them to get involved in discussion and decision making about their service.

5 Describe your views on coaching and mentoring. Do you find them useful tools?

Coaching and mentoring are both highly effective tools. All new starters within the department are assigned a member of staff as a mentor for support, and I would like to think that informal mentoring is continually taking place among colleagues. Although it is not strictly a form of mentoring, we encourage a lot of job shadowing within the department as a development strategy for staff to acquire the new skills required within a newly converged service. For example, staff who were formerly traditional library assistants now find themselves in a position where they may be doing audiovisual set ups within teaching rooms. This type of change has been achieved through shadowing colleagues and using informal mentoring as a support mechanism.

Through the type of transformation that the college and the department have recently experienced, all staff have been required to develop new skills and roles, and this has been achieved, in part, through informal peer-to-peer mentoring.

On a different level, I have been quite proactive in informally (but intentionally) mentoring colleagues who are relatively new to their team management roles. As their line manager, this kind of informal mentoring is achieved through our regular one-to-one review meetings, and often comes in the form of discussion, leading to managerial advice and guidance. Similarly, such meetings offer ideal platforms for coaching to take place, where colleagues have particular issues they need to resolve within their teams. I find it especially fulfilling to see my managers deploying the management skills and solutions to problems they have acquired as a result of informal mentoring and coaching.

The managers and team leaders within the department are all aware of coaching as a technique for problem solving and staff development, and I encourage them to practise and use these skills wherever possible.

6 Can you tell us about a time when you have created and developed a team. What approaches did you use and how did the team respond? What impact did that have on the results of the team?

Creating teams from within existing larger teams can be quite complex. During 2006–7, as e-learning became more important within the college, there was a distinct demand for more staffing to be made available to support the development of e-learning, and in particular digital resources and media within an e-learning context. This coincided with a decrease in demand for traditional library support. Therefore an opportunity arose to redeploy certain learning resources staff who displayed skills and enthusiasm for digital media and e-learning, and to build up this particular side of the service. The formation of the digital media team, within a converged Learning Resources, also allows for individuals to continue to spend time on service points (issue desks and help desks) but to have dedicated time made available for e-learning and digital media developments. The responsibility for this newly formed team was given to the e-learning development manager, allowing for the establishment of a particularly focused team. For the team to develop, it was necessary for them to have substantial projects which they could work on together. I therefore ensured that the team members worked collaboratively allowing for skills to be shared and developed.

There were mixed feelings about the formation of this team, particularly relating to the focus on new developments, and some staff regarded such a change as dismissive of more traditional services. However, regular communication and explanation (through e-mails and meetings, etc.) allowed for the vision and objectives of the team to be shared with everyone. I focused on the fact that it was everyone's responsibility to support the team, as the services they were offering and developing required support from all staff. Again, if you truly believe in the changes being made, and that they are going to have a positive impact on the teaching and learning activity of the college, then the results will follow. Positive results often come in the form of happy customers. I always like to share positive results with all staff who have played a role in supporting particular teams or individuals, and as a result contributed to the continual development of the service.

7 How important do you think hope is when leading people? How do you foster hope in the future?

If you are successful as a leader, you will be demonstrating effective communication with staff, through active listening and formal and informal communication strategies. Also, if you are getting results and customer satisfaction in the projects and services you are leading, this will establish trust and credibility in the things that you do as a leader. This may take some time, as by the very nature of delivering services, projects and targets, you need to have time in order to implement and accomplish them.

If the above personal practices are in place, they can really contribute towards fostering hope for the future. Certainly within the further education sector there is always something threatening imposed on the department, college or sector as a whole by an external influence (e.g. funding, role changes, job freezes, etc.), but if you have a healthy track record of leading your staff successfully and delivering results, you can use this as a basis for reassuring staff about the future.

In brief, if you concentrate on doing a good job during the present, then you will be arming yourself for fostering hope in the future. And I believe hope is very important when leading people.

References and additional reading

Beatty, L. and McGill, I. (1995) *Action Learning: a practitioner's guide*, 2nd rev. edn, London, Kogan Page.

Belbin, R. M. (1981) *Management Teams: why they succeed or fail*, London, Heineman.

Bennis, W. and Nanus, B. (1997) *Leaders: strategies for taking charge*, 2nd edn, London, HarperBusiness.

Brockmeyer, D. (2005) *Seeking Soul in Library Leadership*, Lanham, MD, Scarecrow Press.

Goffee, R. and Jones, G. (2006) *Why Should Anyone Be Led by You?: what it takes to be an authentic leader*, Boston, MA, Harvard Business School Press.

Goleman, D. (1996) *Emotional Intelligence: why it can matter more than IQ*, London, Bloomsbury.

Handy, C. (1993) *Understanding Organisations*, 4th edn, London, Penguin Books.

Herzberg, F. (1966) *Work and the Nature of Man*, New York, Staples Press.

Hooper, A. and Potter, J. (2001) *Intelligent Leadership: creating a passion for change*, London, Random House Business Books.

Kanter, R. M. (2004) *Confidence: how winning streaks and losing streaks begin and end*, New York, Crown Business.

Kermally, S. (2004) *Developing and Managing Talent: a blueprint for business survival*, London, Thorogood.

Kouzes, J. M. and Posner, B. Z. (1999) *Encouraging the Heart: a leader's guide to rewarding and recognising others*, San Francisco, Jossey-Bass.

Kouzes, J. M. and Posner, B. Z. (2003) *Credibility: how leaders gain and lose it, why people demand it*, San Francisco, Jossey-Bass.

Maslow, A. (1954) *Motivation and Personality*, New York, Harper and Row.

Mullins, J. (2005) Are Public Libraries Led or Managed?, *Library Review*, **55** (4), 237–48.

Nicholson, N. (2003) How to Motivate Your Problem People. In *Harvard Business Review on Motivating People*, Boston, MA, Harvard Business Review Press.

Senge, P. (1990) *The Fifth Discipline: the art and practice of the learning organisation*, New York, Doubleday Currency.

Taylor, D. (2002) *The Naked Leader*, London, Bantam Books.

Thomas, N. (ed.) (2004) *The John Adair Handbook of Management and Leadership*, London, Thorogood.

Tuckman, B. C. and Jensen, M. A. C. (1977) Stages of Small Group Development Revisited, *Group and Organizational Studies*, **2** (4), 419–27.

Walker, K. D. (2006) Fostering Hope: a leader's first and last task, *Journal of Educational Administration*, **44** (6), 540–69.

Setting direction and strategy

Learning objectives

After reading this chapter you should be able to:

- ☑ discuss the nature of strategy, and its relationship to leadership
- ☑ understand the role of leaders in setting strategic focus and direction
- ☑ appreciate the role of leaders in shaping values and cultures
- ☑ recognize the importance of managing corporate reputation and image.

Introduction

This chapter aims to encourage you to reflect on the role of the leader in setting direction and strategy. The focus here is not on the strategic planning process itself, but on influencing where the organization is going, and how it is going to get there. Against a backdrop of an understanding of the complex and dynamic nature of strategy, the process starts with the representation of direction in public statements of mission, vision and objectives. But this is only a beginning. Moving forward in the chosen direction, achieving and performing requires management of the implementation of strategy. Two key aspects of such implementation relate to the development and evolution of culture and values, and the management of a strong corporate reputation and images respectively.

Strategy and leadership

Leadership is concerned with influence. One of the key roles of leaders is to create, share and communicate vision. One of the main differentiators between a manager and a leader is that the leader is externally focused, has vision, and looks to the future. This means that leadership is incontestably associated with direction, and strategy, since strategy is concerned with establishing and sharing long term direction. On the other hand the link to management cannot be severed, because strategy is not only developing plans, but making them happen, and that involves resources and their management.

In today's' dynamic environment strategy making is an ongoing process that engages not only top management, but also managers, team leaders and other staff. Leaders need the capacity and the context to allow them to think, plan and act strategically. The wider and ambitious policy agendas to which information organizations are being expected to respond demand visionary leadership, informed decision making, and dynamic strategy-making processes.

This chapter commences with an exploration of the nature of strategy. Johnson and Scholes provide a useful definition: 'Strategy is the direction and scope of an organisation over the long term which achieves advantage for the organisation through its configuration of resources within a changing environment and to fulfil stakeholder expectations' (2002, 10).

This definition derives from a number of aspects of the characteristics of strategic decisions:

1 Strategic decisions and strategy are usually concerned with the long-term direction of an organization.
2 Strategy is usually concerned with strategic advantage, or being able to offer a better value proposition to customers, than competitors can offer.
3 Strategy concerns strategic fit, or the matching of the resources and activities of an organization to the environment in which it operates, in order to achieve maximum strategic advantage.

In turn this means that strategic decisions typically:

◆ are *complex* in nature

◆ are made in situations of *uncertainty and risk*, since predicting the long term future cannot be concerned with certainty
◆ require an *integrated approach* across the organization
◆ have major resource implications
◆ affect a range of operational activities in the organization, and provide the context for operational decisions
◆ drive change within the organization, and within the relationship between the organization and other organizations.

To summarize, strategic management is concerned with establishing fundamental parameters, has long term implications and is organization-wide. This means that strategy making and management is typically ambiguous, uncertain and complex. Hence the need for confident leaders who can negotiate the dilemmas associated with complexity, changing environments and multiple interacting decisions with uncertain outcomes. Such leaders need to be able to assess risk, and make judgements about the level of risk that is appropriate for their organization. If they get it wrong their job, career, credibility and self-confidence may be on the line.

In addition, no decisions about the future of organizations, whether they are small decisions about, say whether to invest in a significant revamp of a library web page, or possibly more significant decisions such as the closure of two site libraries, are made in isolation. For example the closure of the two site libraries may release the resources to run a more state-of-the-art digital library. In addition all organizational decision-making processes are culturally and politically charged. For example, closing the two site libraries will release resources, but the manager involved with this decision will need to manage stakeholders' expectations and desires both within the library and outside. Other departments may see opportunities to bid for the released resources. Staff at the two site libraries, possibly supported by other colleagues in other libraries, may resist the change, users may have views, and senior managers will make decisions on the basis of what they see as the priorities for the organization.

The complex and culturally and politically charged environment of strategy making, coupled with the uncertainty of internal and external factors, means that there is often a difference between what managers plan to happen and what actually happens. *Intended* strategy is an expression of desired strategic direction deliberately formulated or planned by managers. *Realized* strategy, on the other hand, is the strategy actually being followed by an organization in practice. It may be that the realized strategy better meets the organization's objective, or defines a better place for the organization in the marketplace. Big differences between intended strategy and realized strategy can occur with significant changes in leadership and management, organizational structure or marketplace. There is nothing wrong with a mismatch between intended and realized strategy providing that there is an awareness of the difference, and appropriate actions are taken to manage the situation. Much more serious is strategic drift. *Strategic drift* occurs when the organization's strategy (intended or realized) gradually ceases to be an appropriate response to the organization's context and environment.

Strategic focus and direction

Strategic plans and the planning processes associated with them have their roles in sharing the development of strategy and communicating it widely to a wide range of groups of stakeholders. But, as discussed in the last section, strategy making is more than the formal process of writing a strategic plan – it is making things happen at critical points. It involves monitoring environmental and organizational changes, and knowing when to intervene. Strategy making requires judgements on when to follow previously established plans, and when to adapt or even abandon them. It is not about jumping at every new opportunity, it is about being aware of opportunities and evaluating them carefully, but sometimes intuitively rather than analytically, and choosing the right opportunity. Naturally, the more significant a decision might be for an organization the more carefully it needs to be evaluated, but the difficulty is all too often that what initially looks like a relatively minor decision can over the next few years have significant resource or performance implications. For example, the decision to subscribe to a set of business e-journals may appear to be relatively insignificant, but in a context where provision of e-journals to the business school was previously very limited, evidence of use of this resource may lead to a strong case for further investment. This could lead to developing a better resource base for the business school, and supporting its growth and reputation, while also raising the library's profile within the university, and providing opportunities for additional staffing to support the developing activities in the business school. The important point is that when the first 'small' decision is made no one knows where it might lead.

Strategy making, whether it is essentially incremental, as in the example given above, or step-wise, where strategy consists of one or more significant changes or developments, involves an awareness of the factors that influence the best way forward, and how they are changing.

The process of being aware of the environmental context against which strategies unfold is called *environmental scanning*. Environmental scanning involves gathering as much intelligence as possible about the environment. This environment comprises a macro-environment and a micro-environment.

The micro-environment comprises the actors close to the organization that affect its ability to fulfil its objectives, and includes suppliers, marketing intermediaries, customer markets, competitors and publics.

The macro-environment embraces wider social forces that affect the micro-environment; these include demographic, economic, natural, technological, political and cultural forces. Figure 6.1 shows some of the factors in the macro-environment for information services.

Gathering intelligence, and spotting opportunities and long-term trends is essential leadership activity. Leaders are not only good at this; they enjoy it. Not only do they scan and read external and internal documents, figures and other data, but they have effective people networks that help them to interpret a situation. Information managers, as information professionals, should have a predisposition to be good at environmental scanning; they should have little difficulty in identifying sources and judging the authority of the sources, but beyond this leaders also need to exercise analysis and imagination. That is the challenge!

Political factors
Central and local funding decisions for public and national libraries
Funding decisions for higher education
Increases in student numbers in further and higher education
Governmental and institutional controls that suggest that library services should be provided 'free' to the customer.

Economic forces
Changes in income and consumer spending patterns
Subscription rates for journals
Prices of books
Licence fees for bibliographic databases and electronic journals.

Social factors
Age distribution of target market
Changes in educational levels
Changes in family structures
Increases in diversity in relation to ethnicity, race, sexuality and disabilities
Changes in beliefs about the relationship between individuals and society
Diversity of culture, as exhibited through preferences for music, art, drama and literature.

Technological factors
Telecommunications standards and protocols
New software products, such as improved search engine technology
Innovations in telecommunications, including digital television and mobile technologies.

Environmental factors
Sustainability agenda
Availability and depletion of natural resources.

Legal factors
Health and safety legislation
Legislation defining the roles of libraries
Legislation relating to employment
Copyright legislation
Licensing agreements in respect of the use of data downloaded from databases.

Figure 6.1 Factors in the macro-environment for information services

REFLECTION How would you make sure that your environmental scanning ensured that you were aware of all of the key factors in your information organization's environment, given the extent of the list of factors in Figure 6.1?

Direction is often captured in statements of mission, vision, objectives, goals and performance measures. Statements of vision and mission, in particular, need to be relatively stable. This is all the more important in changing environments; as an information organization may be buffeted in terms of its resources and opportunities it is important that it has and retains an overall sense of mission and vision. Before proceeding further it is useful to have some definition. Table 6.1 provides a summary of some of the key vocabulary in this area, with definitions and examples.

Table 6.1 Strategy vocabulary (developed from Johnson and Scholes (2002))

Term	Definition	Example for a public library
Mission	Overriding purpose in line with the values or expectations of stakeholders	To support regeneration, lifelong learning and a better quality of life for individuals and communities
Vision or strategic intent	Desired future state: the aspiration of the organization	To be recognized as an indispensable community service
Goal	General statement of aim or purpose	To enhance the use of the local studies archive for genealogy
Objective	Quantification (if possible) or more precise statement of the goal	To achieve a 20% increase in usage of digital local studies databases in the next year
Values	Statements of beliefs or principles that underpin organizational or professional philosophies	Importance of: reading and literacy, free access to information, social inclusion, privacy and preservation of cultural heritage
Policies	Statements of principles intended to provide a framework for decisions on a continuing basis	Stock management policy; young people's service policy; access policy; reader development policy

Mission and vision statements should be clear declarations of an organization's beliefs about its own nature and distinctive competencies. They should answer the following questions:

1   What are we doing?
2   Who are we doing it for?
3   Why are we doing it?
4   What should we be doing?

Figures 6.2, 6.3 and 6.4 show some mission statements from information organizations. In framing such a statement to instil direction there is a balance to be struck between something catchy and memorable, which is generally short, and a longer statement that might more effectively capture the information service's mission and differentiate it from other organizations. Senior managers have a significant role in framing or approving such statements; they may be one small but very visible measure of their ability to set and articulate a clear direction for their organization.

Mission and vision statements provide a context for the development of goals, objectives, performance measures and strategies.

University of Reading
The purpose of the Library is to support teaching, learning and research in the University, by developing and promoting access to information resources; and also to contribute to the wider world of scholarship and to the transfer of knowledge, by collaborating and co-operating with other organizations.

Manchester Metropolitan University
The Library's Mission is to seek to support the mission and strategic aims of the University by the efficient and effective provision of materials and services to all members of the Institution.

Open University Library
The Library will provide a high quality information service which supports Open University learning, teaching, and research; enable delivery of the University's strategic plan by supporting its business needs and the personal development of all its staff; play a role in the local learning community by working in partnership with other information providers.

Lancaster University Library
The mission of the Library is to provide, maintain and develop library and information services to support the teaching, learning and research of the University.

Southern Cross University Library (Australia)
Our mission is to foster quality learning, teaching and research for the University and its communities through innovative and effective access to resources and excellence in service.

Anglia Ruskin University
The University Library at Anglia Ruskin University supports the University's academic aims and objectives by ensuring that its students and staff have seamless and timely access to a wide range of library services, excellent learning support and high quality information resources.

University of Canterbury Library, New Zealand
To Guide People to the Creation and Discovery of Knowledge.

Figure 6.2 Some university library mission statements

Mission

Our mission is to become the best public library in the world by being so tuned in to the people we serve and so supportive of each other's efforts that we are able to provide highly responsive service. We strive to inform, enrich and empower every person in our community by creating and promoting easy access to a vast array of ideas and information, and by supporting an informed citizenry, lifelong learning and love of reading. We acquire, organize and provide books and other relevant materials; ensure access to information sources throughout the nation and around the world; serve our public with expert and caring assistance; and reach out to all members of our community.

Aims

We intend to provide:

- Services that are understood and valued by the community and result in library use and involvement from the broadest possible spectrum of residents.
- A caring, welcoming and lively cultural and lifelong learning center for the community.
- Outstanding reference, readers' advisory and borrower services that are barrier free for users of all ages, regardless of ethnic background, educational level, economic status or physical condition.
- Collections of enduring value and contemporary interest that are relevant to user needs and readily accessible from every service point.
- A highly trained and competent staff that reflects the rich diversity of our community and that works together to provide responsive service to all users.
- Appropriate technology to extend, expand and enhance services in every neighborhood and ensure that all users have equitable access to information.
- Facilities that are inviting, safe and well maintained and that are available during hours of greatest convenience to users and equitably distributed throughout the City.
- Careful stewardship of the public trust, which ensures accountability and makes the most efficient and effective use of funds, both public and private; fosters collaboration, cooperation and co-location where possible with other agencies; and builds public/private partnerships to enhance services to our users.

Organizational values

Service to our users is our reason for being. Those who need us most should be our highest priority.

- All employees, volunteers and friends of the Library are valued as human beings and for their important contributions to our service.
- We are a learning organization that is open, collegial, and risk-taking; we nurture our talents and each other and constantly reassess our services and methods to adapt to the changing needs of our community.
- We support and defend intellectual freedom and the confidentiality of borrowers' and inquirers' use of the Library.
- All Library services are provided in a nonpartisan and non-judgmental manner that is sensitive to and supportive of human differences.
- Both staff and patrons are encouraged to laugh often and out loud.

Figure 6.3 Linking Mmission, Aims and Values – The Seattle Public Library

We value:

Passion
- Self confident and passionate – about everything we do
- Committed and involved – to and in the process
- Motivated and driven – to achieve the goals
- Aggressive pursuit – of strategic objectives

Excellence
- Customers first
- Continuous improvement
- Willing to embrace change
- Innovative thinking and practices
- Processes that deliver
- State of the art technology
- Energetic, skilled staff
- A collection to die for

Empowerment
- Leading boldly
- Supporting staff to be their best
- Involving staff at all levels
- Respecting and valuing others
- Standing up for our decisions
- Communicating openly
- Being honest and ethical

Success
- Doing what we say we will do
- Can do thinkers
- Achieving outstanding results
- Taking risks and learning

Figure 6.4 University of Canterbury (New Zealand) Library values statement

---

REFLECTION Which of the mission statements in Figure 6.2 do you think is the most appropriate? Why?

Goals are general statements of aims of purpose. Typically they can be further articulated through a series of objectives, and achievement towards goals can be measured in terms of performance measures or indicators. As distinct from mission and vision statements, these can be used by leaders at different levels of the organization in order to articulate more clearly the specifics of the direction that they expect their team to take, within the context of broader mission and vision statements.

The balanced scorecard of goals and performance measures suggests that organizations need to articulate goals and evaluate performance in all four quarters of the scorecard: financial, process, customer and internal. Balanced scorecards acknowledge the need to incorporate short and long term goals, objectives and measures, and to combine qualitative and quantitative measures. Information organizations need to remain financially healthy, to continue to enhance processes that support service delivery (such as cataloguing and licensing arrangements), work on enhancing service delivery, and cultivate the commitment, motivation and development of their staff. Notice that this rounded approach to goals emphasizes that the leader needs to lead and achieve on a variety of different fronts, including those that are concerned with the management and optimization of resources (finance), those that are customer or user facing, and those that are associated with the culture and values of the organization.

Objectives are a more precise statement of the goal, which make it easier to identify action towards the goal and to measure progress and performance. Objectives are statements of specific outcomes that are to be achieved. Objectives should be *SMART*:

◆ *specific*, or focused, giving details of services and target groups
◆ *measurable*, or quantifiable
◆ *achievable*, within the contexts and resources available
◆ *relevant*, in that they contribute to organizational success, and are aligned with corporate objectives
◆ *timely* so that actions are taken at the right time to achieve market success; this involves judging market readiness.

Shaping values and cultures
Organizational cultures and leadership

Leaders need to work through the culture of their organization. Culture determines how things are done within an organization. Founders of organizations often dictate culture with its associated values. But culture is no easy thing to change, so a less transformational leader may learn to work with and through the organizational culture, influencing culture as they go, but not expecting a radical shift. There are different schools of thought about whether culture can be changed, which derive from the basic definition of culture. So, it is useful to visit some of the ideas about what culture is, in order to understand the challenges in shaping culture and some of the approaches that have been proposed for influencing culture. There is no doubt that in any given organization some aspects of culture are more embedded than others. A good leader spends time working out what they can change and what they can't change.

The earlier sections of this chapter have focused on the leader's role in establishing strategy and direction. Organizational culture is central to the way in which an organization and its members work together to achieve the organizations' objectives. Organizational culture has a significant impact on the experience of working in an organization, on how the organization is perceived by customers and other stakeholders, and on organizational performance. Just as with leadership style, there has been considerable academic and practitioner debate about how best culture can be characterized, and further which types of organizational cultures are appropriate under which circumstances. Indeed, the concept of organizational culture could be regarded as 'contested'. Nevertheless, there is no doubt that a leader must seek to influence followers' work experience, as well as individual, team and organizational performance, and one of the mediators in this is the elusive and slippery set of understandings about how people work together, otherwise described as organizational culture. Accordingly, we introduce some definitions and models of organizational culture to assist in reflection of the leader's role in influencing organizational culture.

What is organizational culture?

First a definition: 'Organizational culture is the collection of relatively uniform and enduring values, beliefs, customs, traditions and practices that are shared by an organization's members, learned by new recruits and transmitted from one generation of employees to the next' (Huczynski and Buchanan, 2007, 623).

One of the most widely quoted and most useful models of organizational culture is Schein's model of culture (as in Figure 6.5), which suggests that there

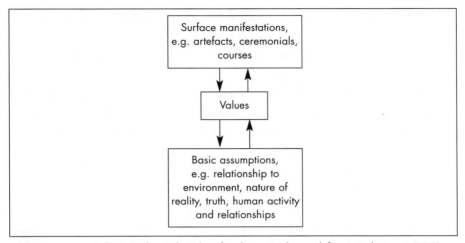

Figure 6.5 Schein's three levels of culture (adapted from Schein, 1985)

are three levels of culture: surface manifestations, values and basic assumptions, and that these three levels interact. Importantly, this model differentiates between surface manifestations which may be managed and manipulated by managers and leaders, and basic assumptions and sharing of meanings among organizational employees, which are more difficult to change or shape. Nevertheless, Schein (1985) suggests that managers and leaders can influence these basic assumptions if they understand what culture is and how it operates.

Surface manifestations of culture are the artifacts, ceremonials and courses that can be seen, heard or felt. Surface manifestations are tools that can be used to challenge and shift culture. On the other hand, although surface manifestations are a good place to start with culture change, leaders need to recognize that culture change is a long process, and changes in surface manifestations should not be seen as a substitute for a genuine long term change in culture. Surface manifestations send a message to the organizations, visitors, customers and most importantly employees. Examples of surface manifestations are:

◆ artefacts, such as tools, furniture and clothes (e.g. uniforms and 'workwear')
◆ ceremonials and rites that recognize achievement or promote a sense of community and belonging

◆ courses, which are used to educate new members through induction and training
◆ heroes and characters who personify the values and beliefs of the culture and offer role models
◆ language, which uses the terms used to convey meaning to others, e.g. staff may be called team players, account executives, library assistants, information technicians or user support officers, all of which send messages about roles and status
◆ norms or expected modes of behaviour that are accepted as the organization's ways of doing things.

Other types of surface manifestations of culture are gestures, jokes, legends, mottoes, physical layout, sagas, slogans, stories and symbols.

REFLECTION What terms are used to describe the roles of staff in your information service? What do these terms convey about the culture of the information service?

Intermediating between surface manifestations of culture and the basic assumptions are organizational values. Values are things that are important to the organization. Values are often unspoken, but are deeply embedded in the basic assumptions within an organization. A leader entering an existing organization can learn a lot by trying to understand key values held by its members. Further, values are often a key source of conflict between sub-groups (such as different departments), and a manager or leader in a non-management role will be much more effective in influencing and attracting followers if they understand and are sensitive to the value sets associated with different groups and sub-cultures and any potential areas for conflict arising from these value sets.

REFLECTION Why might a team of technical resources staff involved with systems, cataloguing, digital archiving etc. have a different set of values from those held by a team of user service advisors in a university library?

Approaches to changing culture

Leaders need to seek to influence the alignment between the organization's culture and its chosen strategy. In particular, in today's dynamic environments the emphasis is the creation of a culture that anticipates and responds to change.

One of the most successful ways of changing culture is not to try to change culture alone, but to seek to change culture as part of a bigger change programme. Restructuring and redefinition of job roles, a new building which requires people to work differently, a new shift pattern, the implementation of a new service and downsizing may all change people's role, the skills required of them, and the other members of staff with whom they interact. This challenges their 'comfort zones' (notions of who they are and what they can do) and their 'cliques' (the people with whom they identify, gossip and exchange mutual support). Culture becomes much more fluid during such a change process, and a good leader will embrace this opportunity not just to change the operational details, but to change people's view of their contribution, to embed new values, expectations, rites and rituals. This sounds easy, but in reality such opportunities for culture change are often either not taken at all, or occur unconsciously on the part of the manager. Even managing operational change can be very demanding and exhausting for a manager. Some managers do embed new values and elements of culture unconsciously, because as they change staff roles, staff who embrace the values that they espouse (e.g. being flexible, good with customers, imaginative, independent, good team workers) may be given more pivotal roles than those who share fewer common values and their associated traits. Lack of attention to culture change in change situations is dangerous because it generates a vacuum. On the other hand this vacuum may be the opportunity for the leader who is not a manager to intervene and influence culture.

Another aspect of the process associated with the formation of culture is the *organizational socialization* process that new members of staff undergo when they join an organization. Through organizational socialization new members of staff (or people who have been moved to different groups) learn what is acceptable to the organization and group, and adapt their pattern of behaviour, values, attitudes and motives in order to conform. There are both formal and informal aspects of organizational socialization, and the wise leader understands both of these elements and how they interact. Formal socialization is typically the responsibility of the human resources function and is achieved, for example, through organizational documentation, mission statements, job descriptions, manuals, induction processes, reward schemes, and training courses. The informal processes occur in the work team through day-to-day interactions with colleagues, mentoring arrangements, role models and exposure to the folklore (stories and myths) of the organization.

REFLECTION Think of a change situation that has been managed by someone else. Did the organizational culture change as a result of the change? If not, why not? If it did, in what way did it change and why?

Leading corporate reputation
The importance of corporate reputation

Values are central not only to culture, but also to reputation, corporate identity and branding. Corporate values as embedded in the culture are a key aspect of corporate identity, or what the organization believes it should be. In order to achieve success the organization must communicate and live those values as it interacts with its customers and other stakeholders. It must not only know what it is about, but it must convince others that it is capable of delivering. To couch this in more practical terms, the public library staff may believe that they have a contribution to make to enhancing the information access in their community, but if others see the library as a store for out-of-date books, then the library will not be very successful. In order to make the contribution that it seeks, it needs to take measures to 'manage' other people's perceptions, or in other words to manage its 'corporate image' and 'corporate reputation'. Leaders have an important role in building and maintaining corporate reputation, which embraces:

◆ *formulating the promise* – or working through corporate values and mission as discussed above
◆ *making the promise* – or communicating and working on the marketing of the message, including considerations of corporate branding and protecting the reputation through public relations
◆ *delivering on the promise* – or ensuring that service delivery and other elements of interactions with stakeholders are professional.

In other words, establishing and maintaining a strong and positive corporate reputation requires alignment between what the organization is seeking to do and is, what it says it does and is, and what it actually does and is.

Defining and discussing corporate reputation

Balmer and Greyser (2006) develop these perspectives further in their discussion of corporate marketing. As summarized in Table 6.2, they propose the six Cs of corporate marketing, and thereby define some relationships between corporate identity and corporate reputation. Notice that this model draws together culture and communication, and the promise or covenant that is implicit in corporate branding. In addition it points to the issue of stakeholders, which we shall return to shortly. Chun (2005) develops this discussion further, suggesting that different academic and professional disciplines have seen corporate reputation as having different meanings; in particular the relationship between concepts of corporate identity, corporate image, corporate reputation and corporate branding is confused. Here we are not concerned with academic debate but rather to draw out some conceptual clarity which might lead to a clearer view of corporate reputation.

Table 6.2 The six Cs of corporate marketing (based on Balmer and Greyser, 2006)

Character	Corporate identity	What we indubitably are
Communication	Corporate communication	What we say we are
Constituencies	Marketing and stakeholder engagement	Whom we seek to serve
Covenant	Corporate brand management	What is promised and expected
Conceptualizations	Corporate reputation	Who we are seen to be
Culture	Organizational identity	What we feel we are

Chun (2005) identifies three schools of thought in the literature on corporate reputation, which differ mainly in the stakeholders that are being considered. A brief review of these approaches is therefore useful to emphasize the different stakeholder groups that are in contention where corporate reputation is concerned. Chun identifies the following schools of thought on corporate reputation:

◆ *the evaluative school*, in which reputation is seen as the evaluation of organizational financial achievement, and performance; the key audiences are the investors and managers

◆ *the impressional school*, in which reputation is seen as the overall impression of an organization; this school tends to see reputation in terms of the relevant stakeholder's perceptions or impression of the organization; major stakeholders in this context are employees and/or customers; image, identity and personality are terms used by the impressional school

◆ *the relational school*, in which reputation is seen as a synthesis of the opinions, perception and attitudes of an organization's stakeholders including employees, customers, suppliers, investors and community. Since taking this position means that corporate reputation is a collective and multi-dimensional construct, the organization does not have a single reputation.

Developing from the position taken by the relational school, Chun (2005) argues that corporate reputation should be used as an umbrella construct, referring to the cumulative impressions of internal and external stakeholders, with image being the external view of the organization, and identity being the internal view. Importantly, also the multidimensional view does not support a simple evaluation of reputation on a scale ranging from good to bad, but rather argues that it is important to be able to profile an organization's reputation on a number of dimensions. One interesting contribution to this field is offered by Davies et al. (2003) in their instrument for measuring corporate reputation. This instrument can be used to measure both identity and image, and thereby to assess any difference between them. The inventory asks stakeholders to assess the organization in terms of its personality. Table 6.3 shows the factors, facets and items in Davies et al.'s corporate character scale, and offers some insight into how corporate character can be described.

Building corporate brands and corporate image

Brands are central to the process of building an image of the organization in the minds of stakeholders. The task of the brand builder is to tease out and

Table 6.3 Seven dimensions of the corporate character scale (based on Davies et al., 2003)

7 factors	14 facets	49 items
Agreeableness	Warmth Empathy Integrity	Cheerful, pleasant, open, straightforward Concerned, reassuring, supportive, agreeable Honest, sincere, socially responsible, trustworthy
Competence	Conscientiousness Drive Technocracy	Reliable, secure, hardworking Ambitious, achievement-orientated, leading Technical, corporate
Enterprise	Modernity Adventure Boldness	Cool, trendy, young Imaginative, up-to-date, exciting, innovative Extrovert, daring
Chic	Elegance Prestige Snobbery	Charming, stylish, elegant Prestigious, exclusive, refined Snobby, elitist
Ruthlessness	Egotism Dominance	Arrogant, aggressive, selfish Inward-looking, authoritarian, controlling
Machismo	NA	Masculine, tough, rugged
Informality	NA	Casual, simple, easy-going

communicate brand values or a brand personality that takes the organization where it wants to go, while building on any existing corporate reputation elements either from internally driven brand identity or from previously established brand image. Leadership is necessary in ensuring that brand building moves the brand forward and does not leave the brand image lingering in its past; on the other hand, too ambitious a leap forward can lead to rejection of the brand on the basis of lack of credibility.

Kotler et al.'s (2005) definition of a brand is worth reiterating: 'A brand is a name, term, sign, symbol or design, or combination of these intended to identify the goods or services of one seller or group of sellers and to differentiate them from those of competitors' (2005, 549).

A brand can be viewed as the organization's promise to consistently deliver a set of benefits and service to customers. The brand supports the consumer in selecting those organizations they will engage with or products they will buy without undergoing a detailed analysis of the potential of that organization or product to deliver what the customer requires. The brand sits at the heart of the relationship between the organization and its customers, and its purpose is to facilitate the process of attracting and retaining a loyal customer base. Brands are much more than their visual design; they symbolize various characteristics of an organization or a product, such as quality, reliability or professionalism, and thereby 'represent' the organization. They add credibility and authority to the whole range of marketing communication approaches, from advertising, sponsorship and personal selling to public relations and e-marketing. Reciprocally, their use in these arenas enhances brand awareness and visibility, and impacts on brand associations. Just as a book is known by its title and/or author, an organization is known by its corporate brand.

Conclusion

Leaders know the importance of understanding, communicating with and influencing stakeholders. Corporate reputation, identity and image, and their representation in brands, are important and the wise leader guards and protects them jealously. This section has offered some perspectives in this area which should link back to mission, vision and other statements relating to strategic direction discussed in the earlier part of this chapter. It has also laid the foundations for the final chapter, which focuses on influencing beyond the information service, or, in other words, impacting and shaping the environment in which the information service finds itself.

Summary and conclusions

One of the most important roles of the leader is associated with setting direction and strategy. This involves not only engaging in formal strategic planning processes, and communicating their outcomes to others, but also in engaging with the processes in organizations that determine what really happens. An awareness of the difference between intended and realized strategy is important, as is a proactive approach to environmental scanning. Equally important is an awareness of the importance of culture and values in determining the way in which plans and strategies are implemented. Schein's three level model of organizational culture, with its concepts of surface manifestation, values and basic assumptions, is helpful in understanding the essential nature of organizational culture and the difference between organizational climate and culture.

Finally, the chapter visited the concept of corporate reputation, and the associated notion of corporate character. These concepts provide a useful link between organizational values and the identity that the organization seeks to project to its stakeholders. This discussion is a useful basis for further discussion on influencing beyond the information organization as discussed in Chapter 8.

Review questions

1   What do you understand to be the link between strategy and leadership?
2   What is environmental scanning and why is it important?
3   Explain the difference between a mission statement, a vision statement, a goal and an objective. Use some examples.
4   Explain and discuss Schein's model of organizational culture.
5   Discuss how leaders may seek to influence and change culture.
6   Why is corporate reputation important?
7   Summarize the different perspectives on corporate reputation adopted by different schools of thought. What is meant by corporate character?
8   What is a brand, and why are brands an important part of strategy?

Challenges

1   Can non-managers really influence strategic direction?
2   How can organizations communicate their strategic direction to staff in an ever changing and uncertain environment in which strategy unfolds and emerges rather than is planned?.
3   What level of overlap should there be between the mission statements of different information services?
4   Is it possible to articulate and understand the value sets held by organization members (as opposed to those that managers would like people to espouse)?
5   Is it possible to change organizational cultures sufficiently quickly to adapt to dynamic environments?
6   Do organizations really have a corporate character?

Case study interview with Caroline Williams, Executive Director, Intute, UK

Context

In 2003 the Joint Information Systems Committee (JISC) was funding eight internet gateways or hubs within a collective named the Resource Discovery Network (RDN). Their brief was to identify and collect the best websites relevant to university and college work. The teams of people who developed the hubs were dispersed geographically across UK education institutions. They worked on different subject areas and had unique identities. They had their own websites, databases, leaflets, plans, strategies and targets. But JISC was concerned; it wanted more value for money. In other words, it wanted the RDN to be used more, to be more widely known and to cost less. The RDN needed to change.

The first step in the change process was the creation of an executive based within Mimas, the national data centre at the University of Manchester. In October 2004 I was appointed as Executive Director and the transition began. We changed the organizational structure, we integrated the technologies and databases, and we undertook a strategic rebrand exercise and re-created our performance measurement framework. This culminated in the launch of one new organization and service, Intute, on 13 July 2006. Intute offers internet search tools, training materials and personalization and community tools.

The role of the Executive Director

My role is to provide the strategic lead for Intute. I manage the Executive and manage the Intute programme of work including acting as project sponsor for additional projects (which attract further funding). I am the main contact between Intute and JISC and represent the service at Board meetings. The Executive provides the mechanisms of accountability to JISC in financial terms and for performance measurement and monitoring.

I have an MA in Library and Information Studies, a MBA (Open) 2006, and am a MSP (Practitioner). Prior to this role I have had a variety of positions in UK university libraries, including Library Service Manager (Electronic Service Development) at the Manchester Metropolitan University Library.

1   What is the most difficult aspect of keeping up to date with key developments within your organization and beyond that might affect the strategy for your information service?

When I first took up post I undertook a detailed analysis of the environment within which the organization operated. I wanted to find out everything I could about my new organization and its context. So I met with staff; I asked questions like 'What do you do, who are your users, and what do they want?' I read dense technical reports about search engines, portals, enterprise systems and digital libraries. I found out about similar services in other countries. I read past reviews and analysis, and looked at statistics of students by subject.

Once completed, the analysis formed the basis for a new organizational vision and strategy, without which it would have been impossible to move forward. The vision was grounded in the environmental analysis but was kept deliberately general rather than detailed so that it could survive as the context changed. The strategy was clear and certain in its aims for improved communication, technical consolidation, better performance measurement and renewed focus on stakeholder needs. However, to realize the strategy it became apparent that as an organization made up of eight separate entities, we would be faced with significant barriers. It looked likely that the barriers would be in communication, decision making and technical standardization. Ultimately, our existing organizational structure and ways of working would not maximize the benefits of the service to users.

Since then (2003), scanning literature and talking to stakeholders is in some instances systematic and in others more ad hoc. The Intute Management Board provides access to strategic thinkers on a quarterly basis. Policy Strategy Forum meetings and Executive visits to the partner institutions keep me in touch with people managing and creating different aspects of the service who are close to their user communities. Relationships with key members of JISC have been established and information exchanged in line with their committee meeting cycle but also more informally 'as and when'. The emphasis on different aspects of the strategy tends to shift according to informal and ad hoc information.

We did a complete rewrite of the strategy in November 2006 as part of the process of writing the Intute business case, business plan and strategic technical development plan (at the request of JISC). Creating the business case required a lot of research, evidence collection and analysis. It was used to validate the ongoing viability of our programme of work, and it was crucial to get this right in order to secure ongoing funding. We commissioned a series of 'strategic stakeholder' interviews and ran a survey of academic use of the Internet. Technical staff undertook an analysis of the technical environment, other staff developed scenarios of use attributable to different user groups, and others looked closely at internet research skills and information literacy. Everything was scrutinized. We went back to our 'unique selling point', core competencies and capabilities, and asked ourselves 'does this remain valid?'. Our university library supporters allowed us to quote their financial savings accrued by using Intute (as opposed to creating and maintaining subject lists of recommended websites themselves), and we attempted to quantify our benefit to the community. We built up a body of evidence and reflected on our strategy and vision . . . and we changed it. The business case and plan, new strategy and vision, and strategic technical development plan were submitted to JISC and we received confirmation of success with a commitment to a further five years of funding.

2   What are the stages in the strategic planning process in your organization?

In the past, as described above, the stages around strategic planning can be summarized as follows: request from JISC; Executive analysis of environment; consultation and input from Intute partners and Board; finalize by Executive; approval by Board; submission to JISC; approval/feedback from the JISC Content Services Committee (JCS); turn strategy into plans (create/edit blueprint, create/edit internal project briefs); carry out work; review progress; revise blueprint.

We have not yet established regular reviews of the strategy, although we review the blueprint (our master plan) every six months. It is likely that we will use our PSF meetings to review the strategy biannually and move towards a bottom up creation of strategy. We do not anticipate a review from JISC until 2009, so do not expect such a top down impetus over the next two years.

3   What have been your biggest challenges in leading a strategic planning process? How did you overcome them?

The vision underpinning Intute was one of unification. A successfully managed unification was essential at a number of levels. I felt this was very successfully and intuitively handled by the Executive. Personally I greeted the new Intute with a huge sigh of relief, as it was the only road to survival. But it was knife edge stuff. The powerful collective identity we have now was born in the most difficult times. I would like to remember the first time we all started talking about 'we'; that was the turning point. 'We' is one of our most frequently used words.

To my mind the strategic process in the beginning (2003–4) was like walking a tightrope between the hub cultures, priorities, identities, resources and capabilities and the changing environment, all compounded by the need for unification to realize synergy and economies of scale, and so build a strong foundation for the future. Different people had different views on the direction they should go in; I had to harness this into discussions about the direction 'we' should go in. I did take a top down approach which seemed to be the right way forward at the time, but is not the way I would like to operate in future. The approach, however, was grounded in detailed analysis and inclusive discussions. It forced us to learn the difference between consultation and consensus. The time and range of communication skills required was significant. I had to pay attention to detail as well as the big picture. This proved to be demanding and psychologically taxing over a period of 18 months; it required resilience and persistence.

4 Does your organization and/or your information service have a mission statement – if so, what is it, and how is it used?

Intute has a mission and vision which is the starting point for the strategy, which is then translated into the blueprint (master plan). This is all in line with the Office of Government Commerce's (OGC's) Managing Successful Programmes (MSP) approach. The role of the Blueprint is to outline the characteristics of the 'future state' we are working towards. Ours is 24 pages long and is arranged in groupings of activity under each strategic aim. It contains details of 23 projects (four of which have attracted additional funding) and specifies what we were hoping to achieve at breakpoints in five tranches from 2007 to 2009. Project briefs are written and management of the projects divided between all available managers. This all works well in practice; staff are clear about their roles and they understand how their work fits in to the big picture. Delegation is improved and there is a clearer understanding of what was required from everyone by when, which is vital in a geographically distributed service. Figure 6.6 shows our mission and aims.

5 What are the core values espoused by your organization?

We do have core values which we share internally; these are summed up in what we

Mission
We exist to advance education and research by providing quality assured services that promote the best of the web. Our service is continually positioned to enable the education and research community to unlock knowledge from the internet with confidence.

Vision
Our vision is to create value by bringing together human expertise and advancing technology in response to community needs that we understand. Innovation, knowledge creation and collaboration are central to our vision of being an authoritative mentor for UK further and higher education.

Strategic aim 1
Ensure that Intute supports the strategies of key national stakeholders including DfES, HE funding councils and research councils by offering a service that is clearly differentiated from search engines and other internet services. Differentiation is possible partly through active collaboration to ensure services are not duplicated and partly by staying ahead of the competition through the use of innovative partnerships and alliances.

Strategic aim 2
Demonstrate and quantify the value of Intute to the HE and FE community and deliver cost savings to individual institutions through the economies of scale provided by Intute as a national service.

Strategic aim 3
Discover and promote quality-assured internet resources, and advance the discerning and effective use of the internet by staff and students in further and higher education.

Strategic aim 4
Establish and maintain a service that embraces the innovative use of internet technologies in the academic environment.

Strategic aim 5
Secure the future of Intute by establishing a business model that is efficient and sustainable, building on the human assets of Intute as a centre of expertise and without compromising on the mission and vision of Intute.

Figure 6.6 Mission, vision and strategic aims: where we want to be

call the 'authorative mentor' which is the basis of our brand vision. Again, with the help of an external consultancy we were able to identify, discuss, agree and articulate all this. We have done further work on articulating our key messages (which we keep refining) and use them for communication with different audiences.

Key messages: best of the web for education and research; for the community by the community; innovation; sustainability and value for money.

6 Can you give some examples of the surface manifestations of the culture of your information service? To what extent are these manifestations shared throughout the parent organization of which your service is part?

Many manifestations relate particularly to the 'for the community by the community' and 'innovation' key messages, i.e. we try to practise what we preach. For example, we:

- have a number of partner institutions (7) and their partners (70) involved in creating Intute, and there is extensive consultation and communication between partners
- are working with JIBS to form an Intute JIBS enhancement group
- have an internal project to integrate Intute in university websites, library catalogues and websites etc.

Further manifestations of our culture include:

- being about to commission an external piece of market research, i.e. we are listening to our users and potential users
- feedback links welcoming feedback from our users
- having a site with links welcoming contributions from our users
- academic subject groups arranging our website in line with university practice (i.e. faculties, schools, departments)
- the style (design and copy) of our publicity and promotional materials including press releases
- attending conferences and giving conference presentations
- embracing technology, manifested in our presence in Second Life, our blogs, podcasts and MyIntute.

Publicity and communication work is shared in some instances with Mimas, press releases appear on the JISC website and we have open channels of communication with the JISC communication team. Partner institutions tap into the dissemination routes within their institutions. Logos provide links to and from websites of all partners.

7 What measures do you take to develop or protect the reputation of your organization?

I interpret reputation as image, consistency and sincerity, i.e. as an organization we aim to do what we say we'll do from whichever angle we are approached. Therefore everyone and all 'views' of Intute, e.g. website, publicity material, e-mails etc., should adopt the same principles and a similar tone and design. In order to realize this we've invested in staff development and training and internal stakeholder management, as well as holding regular internal management and team meetings (for collective decision making, information sharing and consultation). From an outward facing perspective we conduct a blog watch and a media watch to track mentions of Intute, and manage our relationships with key stakeholders, in particular funders. The latter in practice often leads us to align ourselves with strategies of other organizations.

References and additional reading

Alvesson, M. (2002) *Understanding Organizational Culture*, London, Sage.

Balmer, J. M. T. and Greyser, S. A. (2006) Corporate Marketing: integrating corporate identity, corporate branding, corporate communication, corporate image, and corporate reputation, *European Journal of Marketing*, **40** (7/8), 730–41.

Chun, R. (2005) Corporate Reputation: meaning and measurement, *International Journal of Management Reviews*, **7** (2), 91–109.

Cohn, J. M., Kelsey, A. L. and Fiels, K. M. (2002) *Planning for Integrated Systems and Technologies: a how-to-do-it manual for librarians*, 2nd edn, D. Salter (ed.), London, Facet Publishing.

Corrall, S. (1998) Scenario Planning: a strategic management tool for the future, *Managing Information*, **5** (9), 34–7.

Corrall, S. (2000) *Strategic Management of Information Services: a planning handbook*, London, Aslib.

Davies, G., Chun, R., DaSilva, R. and Roper, S. (2003) *Corporate Reputation and Competitiveness*, London, Routledge.

Deal, T. E. and Kennedy, A. A. (1982) *Corporate Cultures: the rite and rituals of corporate life*, Reading, MA, Addison-Wesley.

Evans, G. E., Layzell Ward, P. and Rugaas, B. (2000) *Management Basics for*

Information Professionals, Oxford, Neal-Schuman.

Galliers, R. D., Baker, B. S. H. and Leidner, D. E. (2002) *Strategic Information Management: challenges and strategies in managing information systems*, Chicago, Butterworth-Heinemann.

Hannagan, T. (2002) *Mastering Strategic Management*, Basingstoke, Palgrave.

Himmel, E. and Wilson, W. J. (1999) *Planning for Results: a public library transformation process*, Chicago, American Library Association.

Huczynski, A. A. and Buchanan, D. A. (2007) *Organizational Behaviour*, 6th edn, Harlow, FT Prentice Hall.

Johnson, G. and Scholes, K. (2002) *Exploring Corporate Strategy*, 6th edn, Harlow, FT Prentice Hall.

Kotler, P., Wong, V., Saunders, J. and Armstrong, G. (2005) *Principles of Marketing*, 4th European edn, Harlow, FT Prentice Hall.

Mason, M. G. (2000) *Strategic Management for Today's Libraries*, Chicago, American Library Association.

Nelson, S. (2002) *The New Planning for Results: a streamlined approach*, Chicago, American Library Association.

Orna, E. (1999) *Practical Information Policies*, Aldershot, Gower.

Pantry, S. and Griffiths, P. (2000) *Developing a Successful Service Plan*, London, Library Association Publishing.

Pettigrew, A. M. (1979) On Studying Organizational Cultures, *Administrative Science Quarterly*, **24** (4), 570–81.

Robson, W. (1997) *Strategic Management and Information Systems: an integrated approach*, 2nd edn, Harlow, FT Prentice Hall.

Rowley, J. (2006) *Information Marketing*, 2nd edn, Aldershot, Ashgate.

Schein, E. H. (1985) *Organizational Culture and Leadership*, San Francisco, Jossey-Bass.

Ward, P. L. (2003) Management and the Management of Information, Knowledge-Based and Library Services 2002, *Library Management*, **24** (3), 126–50.

Weissinger, T. (2003) Competing Models of Librarianship: do core values make a difference?, *Journal of Academic Librarianship*, **29** (1), 32–9.

7

Leadership development

Learning objectives

After reading this chapter you should be able to:

- ☑ appreciate the need for investment in leadership development, particularly in a LIS context
- ☑ understand the diversity of ways in which individuals learn
- ☑ understand the different models and theories associated with leadership development approaches
- ☑ understand the benefits of coaching and mentoring in this context
- ☑ critically assess leadership programmes and their value
- ☑ begin to consider applying these approaches to leadership development for yourself and for others
- ☑ understand the concept of the learning organization.

Introduction

Developing leadership potential and capacity across the library and information sector has been touched on throughout this book. This chapter takes an in-depth, detailed and holistic look at leadership development primarily because we believe it is a fundamental consideration for library organizations, managers and information professionals at all levels. The chapter begins by asking why leadership development is so important; it then moves on to explore the diversity of ways in which individuals learn, drawing on Kolb's learning cycle theory, Honey and Mumford's learning styles and Armstrong's theory of multiple intelligences. Models and theories of leadership development are illustrated, including a focus on coaching and mentoring within the context of building leadership capacity. Leadership development programmes for the library and information profession are explored and evaluated in some detail, with specific examples provided to illustrate approaches and impact. The chapter then moves on to consider approaches to leadership development for ourselves as individuals, and for others. The chapter ends by introducing the concept of the learning organization and what this means for libraries and leadership development.

Why leadership development?

In Chapter 1 we described the underlying philosophy of this book, highlighting that learning must be at the heart of what we do as leaders and future leaders. We also stressed that we must spend time on leadership development from the start of our careers and at whatever stage. Irrespective of role, leaders should be striving to improve practice and to learn from others. As leaders we must also think about how our staff can improve, develop and deploy their leadership abilities. Chapter 2 emphasized the importance of self-knowledge, of knowing yourself as a leader; this is only the start of the journey as we take this self-awareness and plan for our own leadership development, using the best approaches and tools available. Consequently, as individuals we must demonstrate a commitment to our own development and to the development of others.

Many authors considering generic leadership issues believe that there is a problem with leadership development, that despite investment it is still 'not working'. We are conscious that specifically designed leadership programmes are often held up as the 'solution' for developing leaders – the 'answer' to the leadership 'problem'. We suggest that although such programmes are of value and can be very powerful, they are only one option and one part of what should be an ongoing and complex approach to developing leadership abilities and confidence. Many authors have stressed the need for organizations to look to capacity building for leadership, to develop and retain talent, and to create an environment conducive to learning and development. Without this focus on leadership development and learning, library and information services will not be able to create and develop leadership at all levels and consequently cannot hope to meet the challenges they face in the future. This focus on leadership development for the future of the library and information profession was the subject of the IFLA Continuing Professional Development and Workplace Learning section conference in 2007 and the multiple issues, concerns and potential solutions are reflected in the proceedings (Ritchie and Walker, 2007).

Learning must therefore be at the core of current and future leaders' priorities. Bennis and Nanus' (1997) research asked 90 leaders about the personal qualities they felt they needed to run their organizations: 'they talked about persistence and self-knowledge; about willingness to take risks and accept losses; about commitment, consistency and challenge. But, above all, they talked about learning' (175). Learning about ourselves, about leadership, others and the context we work in is therefore crucial for aspiring leaders and existing leaders, 'Very simply, those who do not learn do not long survive as leaders' (Bennis and Nanus, 1997, 176).

REFLECTION Think of a leader you admire; do they continue to 'learn' and how do they do this?

Understanding how we learn: multiple intelligences and learning styles

Any discussion of leadership development is predicated on learning concepts and on understanding how people learn. It is important to understand learning approaches and preferences in order to ensure that we choose how best to learn and so we can provide advice to others. At a basic level, Parsloe and Wray (2000) suggest three questions we need to answer before we can begin to understand what learning approach might suit us:

1   How do you perceive information most easily: do you learn best by seeing, hearing, moving or touching?

2 How do you organize and process the information you receive: are you
   predominantly left brain, right brain, analytical or global?
3 What conditions are necessary to help you to take in and store the
   information you are learning: the emotional, social, physical and
   environmental factors?

Moving on from this, it is helpful to consider learning as a process, a cycle
that we enter at different points depending on the situation we find ourselves
in. The most influential theorist in this arena is Kolb, who described learning
as the process whereby knowledge is created through the transformation of
experience. Kolb's model has four distinct phases, as represented in Figure
7.1. We can enter the model at any stage and it can and should continue
indefinitely as a cycle.

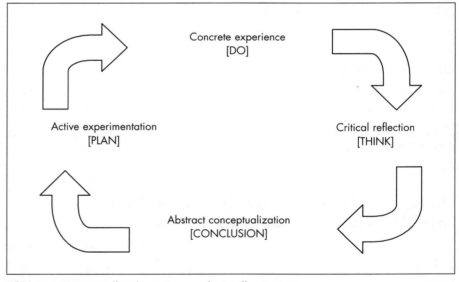

Figure 7.1 Kolb's learning cycle (Kolb, 1984)

REFLECTION What conditions are necessary to help you to take in and store the
information you are learning: the emotional, social, physical and environmental
factors?

Each individual will find some stages of the learning cycle easier than others and this reflects their preferred learning style or styles. Learning style analysis suggests that individuals need to adapt and adjust their preferences to make the most of learning opportunities. Honey and Mumford (1982) are influential theorists in this field and their learning styles questionnaire and model link with Kolb's learning cycle, again helping individuals to identify their preferences and to understand how they learn. Honey and Mumford's four learning styles are summarized in Figure 7.2.

Activists [Experience – DO]
Activists are open-minded, not sceptical. They are usually enthusiastic about everything new. Their philosophy is 'I'll try anything once' and they tend to act first and consider the consequences later. They fill their day with activity. Activists learn best from activities where:

- it's appropriate to have a go
- they are thrown in the deep end
- there is excitement and a range of changing tasks to tackle.

Reflectors [Reflection – THINK]
Reflectors like to stand back and consider experiences, observing them from different perspectives and listening to others before making their own comment. They thoroughly collect data and analyse it, postponing reaching definitive conclusions for as a long as possible. Reflectors learn best from activities where:

- they can stand back from events and listen and observe
- they can carry out research and analysis
- they can decide in their own time and have the opportunity to review what they've learnt.

Theorists [Conclusion]
Theorists adapt and integrate observations into complex theories, thinking through problems step-by-step. They can be perfectionists and are keen on principles, theories, models and systems thinking. Theorists learn best from activities where:

- they are intellectually stretched
- situation has a structure and clear purpose
- they can deal with logical, rational argument
- they are offered interesting concepts.

Pragmatists [Plan]
Pragmatists are keen to try out theories, ideas and techniques to see if they work in practice. They search out new ideas and experiment. They like to act quickly and confidently on ideas and can be impatient. Pragmatists learn best from activities where:

- they can implement what you learn immediately
- they try out and practise techniques
- they see a clear link between the subject matter and a real problem at work.

Figure 7.2 Honey and Mumford's four learning styles

REFLECTION Considering Honey and Mumford's learning styles above, which do you think are your preferred learning styles? What can you learn from this to help your own leadership development?

Experience shows that people learn most effectively if they are aware of their own learning styles and preferences, and if they can choose learning opportunities that suit their preferences. Being aware of our preferences, and the preferences of others, can be a major advantage when considering the best learning opportunities. It can also help us to understand differences between ourselves and our colleagues.

A final learning model to consider, which adds a different perspective to understanding how we learn, is Armstrong's theory of multiple intelligences. Armstrong (1993) argues that we each have seven types of intelligences and have preferences within these. We can work to develop all seven types, and should ideally do so to make us a more rounded learner, open to multiple sources of learning. Armstrong also suggests that anyone involved in training, teaching or giving presentations should be aware of the seven intelligences and should aim to incorporate as many as possible to ensure that individuals are stimulated and connect with them. The seven intelligences are represented in Table 7.1 along with suggested ways that each can be stimulated during a learning experience.

Models and theories of leadership development

Having considered the learning process in broad terms, we will turn to approaches to leadership development and consider their applicability within the library and information context. It should be stressed that most theorists agree that we should take advantage of learning opportunities at all points and in all forms, both formally and informally. The ones explored here are not intended to be comprehensive but to highlight some of the choices available.

Experiential learning

Experiential learning has been defined as the insight that is gained through the internalization of our own or observed experiences (Beard and Wilson,

Table 7.1 Armstrong's seven intelligences

Linguistic	This is the intelligence of words. Individuals who are strong in this area can argue, persuade, entertain or instruct effectively through the spoken word.	Debate, stories, jokes and quotes
Logical	This is the intelligence of numbers and logic. Individuals with this trait have the ability to reason, sequence, think logically and enjoy a generally rational outlook on life.	Charts, graphs, tables, statistics, well-structured linear material that has clear outcomes, quizzes
Spatial	This involves thinking in pictures and images. Highly spatial individuals often have an acute sensitivity to visual details and can easily draw and sketch their ideas.	Video clips, pictures, diagrams, mind maps, the use of colour, changes in space and light
Musical	This is the capacity to perceive, appreciate and produce rhythms and melodies.	Music, video clips, audio, tone of voice
Bodily kinaesthetic	This is the intelligence of the physical self. It includes being able to control your own body movements and handle objects skilfully.	Movement, use of props, practical exercises
Interpersonal	This is the ability to understand and work with other people. People who are high in this intelligence have the ability to view the world from someone else's perspective.	Role play, scenarios, small group work, case studies, question and answer
Intrapersonal	This is the intelligence of the inner self – someone who is strong in this intelligence can easily access their own feelings and has a high level of self-awareness and understanding.	Stories, emotion, feedback, questionnaires, test how they are feeling

2002). Experiential learning theory thus builds directly on the influential work of Kolb. It can therefore be argued that people learn about leading through experience and through learning opportunities that involve participation. As a process of reflection and learning which is supported by colleagues, individuals can learn with and from each other. Rather than learning by telling, as is the case in a talk or a lecture, the learner learns by doing, thinking and internalizing the situation before applying relevant aspects to themselves, influencing their future actions and thoughts. Experiential learning can therefore be extremely powerful.

Experiential learning can be put into practice in multiple ways. In the library and information services context we would recommend experiential learning through general *work experience* and more specifically through *job shadowing.* Work experience can be enabled through opportunities for project work, secondments and opportunities to pursue different assignments within a role or focus on particular problems. It is not enough however, for individuals to simply have these experiences to gain more diverse knowledge; in order for deep learning to take place, individuals must contextualize the experience within the learning cycle and, ideally, be supported through this by their manager or a colleague. An example of this is explored in Figure 7.3.

Anne, a public services team leader in a large public library service, has the opportunity to be seconded to manage a community project aiming to attract more teenagers into the library.

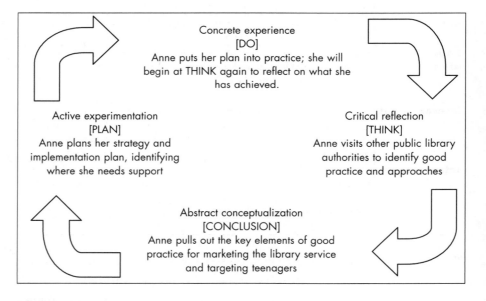

Figure 7.3 Work experience in practice

Throughout this project Anne was supported by her manager who helped her contextualize the project within the wider organization and to apply her learning; her manager also helped her to consider how she wished to develop her career further at the end of the project.

REFLECTION Think of a time when you have learnt from work experience. How could Kolb's learning cycle help to structure and consider the learning process?

The literature on *job shadowing* is predominantly related to the private sector and is commercially oriented. Noting their use as a career progression tool or 'jet fuel', Barbian (2002) and Shakespeare (1994) provide overviews of such schemes with a focus on the benefits but with little reflection on the learning experience, and few in-depth case studies. Holden and McGrath (1992) explore job shadowing's potential for self-development for students on undergraduate courses, identifying the conditions under which the shadow is best equipped to take advantage of the learning opportunity, and stressing the importance of reflection, the examining of how and what is learnt. The consideration of individual needs and match-making are crucial as the success of the approach is dependent on the suitability of the match.

Kolb's sequence of do, think, conclude and plan can be applied with particular relevance to job shadowing. The learner, or shadow, observes and experiences the working day of the host by accompanying them to a variety of meetings and other activities. During this time the learner absorbs the experiences of the host's work. This experience can only be transformed to a deep learning experience by a process of critical reflection whereby the learner contemplates what has been observed and makes assessments about the host's style of work, their interpersonal skills as well as undertaking a situational analysis. All these components need to be shaped into an action plan which the learner can take back to their own work situation. The cycle is then completed when aspects of the plan are implemented in the learner's own job situation or used to further their personal career development.

Job shadowing can be particularly beneficial in a leadership context, either for aspiring senior leaders or for staff at different stages in the organization (for a case study on job shadowing for leadership development see Bruce and Roberts, 2003). Many library and information services have implemented their own job shadowing schemes, and there are also examples of intra-organizational and cross-sectoral schemes that provide opportunities for individuals to shadow roles in different types of organizations and across different library sectors. Examples of this include ALLIS (Accessing Lancashire Libraries and Information Services) in the north west of England, which provides a job shadowing scheme for staff across all members (academic, public and health libraries); see www.allis.org.uk/index.php?p=staffdev for job shadowing scheme guidelines.

REFLECTION Which key elements need to be in place to ensure a successful job shadowing experience within a library and information context? Consider how the ALLIS guidelines could support this process.

Action learning

Action learning is a developmental methodology often used as a part of leadership development programmes. Action learning has been defined as 'a systematic way by which individuals, groups, and organizations learn in the context of real (not simulated) work' (Conger and Riggio, 2007, 72). It is interlinked with experiential learning as it aims to balance the role of action and reflection in order to learn from experience and develop more complex ways of knowing, doing and being. Action learning sets are often established to support individual and group learning, and can be used effectively in a change management context. Action learning initiatives can incorporate projects that address highly complex challenges looking at organization-level change. Many authors recommend that action learning groups have trained facilitators and project sponsors. The leadership development programmes described later in this chapter often use action learning as one methodology.

Rigg and Richards ask 'what is it about action learning that might promise enhanced leadership?' (2006, 2). They do so within the context of public service leadership and development. They describe research which concludes that action learning is more an ethos than a definable method, based on:

- the requirement for action as the basis for learning
- profound personal development resulting from reflection on activities
- working with problems (that have no right answers)
- problems being sponsored and aimed at organizational as well as personal development
- action learners working in sets of peers to support and challenge each other
- the search for fresh questions taking primacy over access to expert knowledge.

Action learning can therefore be seen as directly relevant and beneficial to leadership development as learning is embedded in participants' real problems, as well as being social.

Coaching and mentoring

A brief overview of coaching and mentoring was provided in Chapter 5. As we summarized in that chapter, *Coaching* is a one-to-one approach aiming to develop specific skills in an individual or to enhance performance in some way. Coaching is quite specific in focus and is therefore different from (although often confused with) mentoring. Coaching could be used where an individual has taken on new responsibilities and is struggling with one element, for example project management or managing staff for the first time.

Mentoring is a one-to-one holistic approach to professional and personal development, which can be formal or informal; mentoring involves considering the 'whole person', their career, their skills and what they need in order to succeed. Mentoring is particularly valid for individuals in new roles or who are at key stages in their careers. Mentoring could be used where an individual is at a crossroads in their career, for example a branch library manager who has returned from a career break while having a family and who is feeling unconfident and unsure of the future.

In this chapter, we consider coaching and mentoring in the context of leadership development and learning and focus in more detail on their impact on individuals and organizations. Parsloe and Wray argue that coaching and mentoring have become popular as an answer to the deficiencies that have long been known to exist with traditional training methodologies. They are therefore viewed by many theorists as the 'essential glue that makes training courses stick' (Parsloe and Wray, 2000, 39) and should definitely play a key role in organizations' learning strategies. Parsloe and Wray also cite research which showed that on average only 10–20% of learning through training transfers into people's work. Methods such as coaching and mentoring can facilitate learning and development, and improve performance. There is, however, often confusion with regard to what a coach and mentor do and the two approaches can be applied in the wrong context and haphazardly. Figures

7.4 and 7.5 illustrate the processes of coaching and mentoring and highlight the different stages and applications.

Performance improvement needed
Stage 1: Analysis for awareness (assessment of need)
  Stage 2: Plan for responsibility (agree the plan)
    Stage 3: Implement using styles, techniques and skills
      Stage 4: Evaluate (has performance improved?)

Is performance improvement still required – is further improvement possible? If so, start again!

Figure 7.4 Coaching model (after Parsloe and Wray, 2000)

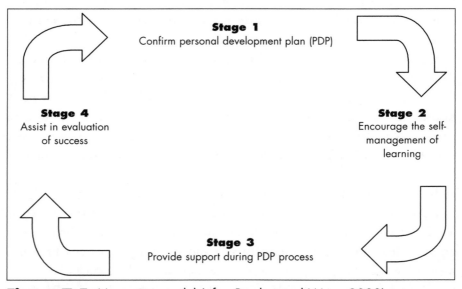

Figure 7.5 Mentoring model (after Parsloe and Wray, 2000)

In a leadership development context within the information services sector, coaching could be used to help a library manager whose team has recently been merged with another team and who is struggling with conflict and tensions, and is unsure of how to create a shared vision for the team. A coach would help the individual to help themselves by listening to the problem, asking probing questions and enabling the manager to develop a plan of action.

In a leadership development context within the information services sector, mentoring could be used to provide a framework for supporting an individual who is participating in a national leadership development programme. The individual would develop a personal development plan, either before the programme or early on, possibly using self-assessment tools to inform it, and would benefit from a mentor to provide support and encouragement throughout the programme and after its conclusion.

REFLECTION Can you identify stages in your career when coaching or mentoring would have been beneficial? Explain why.

Formal programmes

Formal leadership programmes and courses are still widely used to improve leadership in organizations. Leadership training can take many forms and is designed to increase generic skills and behaviours relevant for leadership effectiveness. Training can vary from one-off workshops on particular aspects of leadership such as team development or change management, to comprehensive programmes that last for a year or more. Many large organizations also operate a management/leadership training centre for employees, and individuals can also undertake formal programmes of study such as an MBA. Leadership institutes also provide opportunities for intensive and focused time with a cohort of other learners; these have recently become popular and there are several institutes of relevance to the library and information sector (these are explored later in this chapter). Such institutes often take a specific professional grouping, for example LIS professionals or academic leaders, and use a range of leadership development tools including assessment tools, a taught course element, mentoring, coaching, action learning and peer group networks.

It has been suggested that it is not enough for individuals to attend leadership development courses alone. Research has demonstrated that in order for training to be successful, certain conditions must be in place:

◆ clear learning objectives
◆ clear, meaningful content
◆ appropriate sequencing of content

◆ appropriate mix of training methods (see previous section on learning styles and multiple intelligences)
◆ opportunity for active practice
◆ relevant, timely feedback
◆ trainee self-confidence
◆ appropriate follow-up activities.

Leadership development programmes and institutes for LIS professionals

There now exist a diverse range of leadership development programmes and institutes worldwide targeted at the library and information professional. Some are very specific in their focus, for example public library leaders in the UK, academic library leaders in the USA. Others take a cross-sectoral approach, and some also include a cross-section of related professionals, for example IT and library professionals in higher education. This part of the chapter provides an overview of such programmes, the development approaches they use, and reflects on their impact. Table 7.2 illustrates a range of examples internationally (which are not all necessarily current). The motivation to establish such programmes or institutes is powerfully articulated by Billy Frye (www.fryeinstitute.org):

> Many of the elements that are needed to make a great university are in short supply: money, books and journals for the library, a sound technology base, staff, better supported services. But the resource that is most valuable and in shortest supply is leadership. So as we plan for the future we must make provision for the recruitment and development of potential leaders – persons who are capable of seeing the big picture and understanding institutional relationships: persons who welcome change and have the vision, imagination and courage to take carefully considered risks; and who are unselfish in their goals, fair in their dealings, and trusted by the colleagues at all levels with whom they work.

Table 7.2 Examples of LIS leadership development programmes and institutes

Programme	Country	Target audience	Summary of approach
Northern Exposure to Leadership	Canada	Librarians who have graduated from a library school in the past seven years and have had a least one year of professional experience	Five-day residential for new professionals; highly individualized, drawing on the learner's own history; direct delivery and experiential
Frye Leadership Institute	USA	Those in higher education who aspire to more significant leadership roles, including disciplinary faculty, librarians, information technology professionals and administrators	Two-week residential; personal interaction; direct application to participants' own work contexts
Leading Modern Public Libraries Programme	UK	Public library staff at different levels – heads of service, senior managers and future leaders	Self-assessment using transformational leadership questionnaire; a balance of strategy, theory and practice
SCONUL/ UCISA/British Library Future Leaders Programme	UK	Experienced professional information services staff (typically covering library, ICT and related activities) with proven management experience, to deepen their understanding and leadership ability, and develop their potential	Preparation via self-assessment using Myers-Briggs; action learning based; learning sets established

Although their focus and audiences may differ, the goals and approaches of such programmes are usually similar. The two examples below provide an insight into their focus, purpose and underpinning principles.

Northern Exposure to Leadership (NEL) (taken from Brockmeyer, 2005, 94)

Open to the library profession in general in Canada, this programme's goals are to instill progressive and effective leadership strategies, attitudes and skills by:

◆ providing participants with an individual and personal learning experience in order to build a foundation on which they can develop leadership skills

◆ encouraging participants to recognize and initiate creative innovations and seize opportunity, especially when there is risk involved
◆ guiding participants to appreciate and thrive in a changing political and demographic environment
◆ encouraging individuals to build individual networks
◆ affording the library profession a forum in which to begin to create a community of library leaders.

Leading Modern Public Libraries Programme

Aiming to develop leadership capacity within UK public libraries to meet future needs, the Department for Culture, Media and Sport (DCMS) worked with the Museums, Libraries and Archives Council (MLA) and the Society of Chief Librarians (SCL); they formed a Leadership Steering Group and created a brief for a leadership development programme that would be:

◆ a strategic intervention to deliver the vision of Framework for the Future
◆ national – reaching all library authorities in England
◆ contextualized – a programme which draws on a range of leadership theories and practice but is customized to address the specific leadership issues facing public libraries today
◆ multi-layered – reaching staff who are already heads of services, senior staff who have experience and responsibility for service-wide developments, and staff who are already showing the potential to be future leaders.

REFLECTION Consider the two programmes' goals and approaches above; what are the key features of each and what will be different?

Most leadership programmes include the range of development techniques and approaches explored previously in this chapter and in Chapter 2. They begin with some form of leadership assessment, for example the Myers-Briggs personality team profile, which provides participants with feedback (often 360 degree feedback) and opportunities for self-reflection on personal preferences and leadership styles. There is usually a strong element of peer support with relationships formed either formally through action learning sets or informally. Mentors are also often used and can be drawn from within the library profession or from the professional coaching and training community. Such programmes also incorporate elements of experiential and theoretical learning with the actual curriculum varying according to the particular purpose and audience. For example, the Frye Leadership Institute is aimed at a wide range of potential leaders in higher education; consequently its curriculum encompasses:

◆ perspectives on issues in higher education
◆ innovation in higher education
◆ issues in scholarly communication
◆ teaching and learning
◆ intellectual property: the legal and societal framework
◆ government information policy and its influence on access to information within the university
◆ public policy and higher education
◆ impact of technology on college and university economics, budgeting, and organization
◆ leadership in an era of transformational change.

There are clearly different benefits from attending programmes with differing foci. Programmes that are drawn from one particular library sector bring the advantages of focus, established networks, common vocabulary and challenges. Those that cut across library sectors bring opportunities for learning from a wider base of examples, for developing a diverse network, and providing potential within careers to move across sectors. Programmes like Frye that focus on a particular context but encompass a wider range of professionals (library, IT, academic, administrative, etc.) arguably bring focus, shared context and challenges, plus the opportunity to learn and discuss issues across professional boundaries. Larger organizations (either libraries themselves or their host organizations) are also investing in localized and tailored leadership development programmes. Examples include Victoria University of Wellington's (New Zealand) Leading People

Programme open to all University managers, and Edge Hill University's (UK) Future Leaders and Managers programme aimed at staff within Learning Services (library, IT, media, skills support and e-learning) who wish to develop their leadership potential and management skills.

Participants' reflections on their experiences of such programmes highlight its personal nature, described by one UK professional as the 'first steps on a personal journey' (Stevenson, 2006). The extent of the personal, as well as professional impact, of such programmes is depicted by the following reflection taken from Brockmeyer's research into North American leadership institutes for library professionals:

> The Northern Exposure experience for me was life changing, career affirming and enlightening. The largest impact it left on me was to change the nature of my thinking – I learned the power of positive thinking and afterward I felt that I could do anything with my life or career if wanted to. I suppose it gave me a sense of empowerment that profoundly changed me . . . NEL [Northern Exposure Leadership] came just in the nick of time for me for I was starting to lose my interest in my work . . . I truly feel that my library needs me not only now in my work as a public service librarian, but in a future leadership position (which I am slowly working towards). (2005, 141)

The above reflection clearly demonstrates the life-changing nature of the leadership programme that was, for this individual, far more than an opportunity to develop their knowledge and skills. A second personal reflection of a UK library leadership programme (Figure 7.6) focuses much more on skills and their application in the workplace. Clearly, the impact varies from person to person and depends on context. The reflection in Figure 7.6 has been anonymized and addresses specific questions as part of the formal evaluation of the programme.

REFLECTION Should leadership development programmes be meaningful personal experiences or should they focus on skills?

Leadership development for yourself

As this chapter has demonstrated, there are multiple opportunities available

Why did you decide to attend the programme?
My manager had been on the initiative for senior managers and thought the training would benefit me at this stage in my career. I wanted to reinforce skills I've picked up 'on the job' and combine my experience with more theoretical management strategies and tools.

What did you expect to achieve as a result of attending the programme?
I expected to be stretched intellectually and have my thinking about management challenged. I also wanted to share experience and ideas with colleagues from other services and acquire a better informed and more rigorous approach to problem solving.

Did the programme meet your expectations?
I found the theoretical content excellent and learned an enormous amount from others on the programme. The lessons translate directly to the workplace and the communication styles of both leaders complemented each another excellently. The pace of the course was brisk and focused and the course reader will prove extremely useful in the future.

How do you feel your skills have improved as a result of the programme?
I have learnt to think in a more detached and analytical way, particularly with regard to personality typing, which wasn't something I'd come across before. Understanding the unseen reasons why people behave as they do has helped me deal with situations more clearly and objectively. My manager has noticed this and I feel it's been appreciated by my staff.

Do you feel the training you received has improved the performance of your service more generally?
Although it's relatively soon after the training, I've been able to use some of the techniques I picked up on the programme with managers and staff. In particular, I've tried to introduce group work techniques from the training to our regular meetings. This has led to staff debating and discussing issues in a new and liberated way.

How did the programme compare to other training you've attended?
The training was more 'grown up' than lots of other courses I've attended, with the trainers working on the basis that we knew what we were doing and needed to have our skills honed and improved, rather than developed from scratch. More intellectual rigour was demanded from us than is often the case, with the expectation that we would look at the course reader beforehand and do preparatory work before each of the modules. This made the experience more productive and thought provoking overall.

Figure 7.6 Programme evaluation: example questionnaire and response

to develop your leadership potential and capacity. We each have an individual responsibility for our own learning but the range of methods and programmes can be confusing! It can also be daunting when attempting to assess your own leadership strengths and areas for development. Hernon,

Powell and Young (2003) recommend using a leadership assessment model, arguing that we each possess leadership qualities to varying extents ('it's not a yes or no') and that we need self-assessment plus feedback from others to inform our decision making on leadership development needs. Assessment tools probe an individual's perception of their own performance plus the perceptions of colleagues, peers and staff (for examples see Chapter 2). Other tools recommended for self-assessment include keeping a journal or diary in which to note daily problems, solutions and personal feelings; these can be reflected on later. As we have illustrated here, there are different methods available to help individuals to develop their leadership capacity, and 'there is no single kind of leader-in-training' (Harvard Business Review, 2004, 43). The choice of methods should stem from individual preferences and learning styles.

Many authors stress the importance of gaining support from others – this is important at all stages in our careers and is particularly crucial during significant changes, for example, a move to a leadership position, a personal or professional crisis, changes in responsibility or organization. This support can be as formal or as informal as the individual needs or prefers, and can be gained from a range of colleagues within the information services, within the wider organization, the profession or outside.

Finally, in considering leadership development for yourself, Yukl's (2002) 'Guidelines for self-development of leadership skills' are helpful:

- Develop a personal vision of career objectives.
- Seek appropriate mentors.
- Seek challenging assignments.
- Improve self-monitoring.
- Seek relevant feedback.
- Learn from mistakes.
- Learn to view events from multiple perspectives.
- Be sceptical of easy answers.

REFLECTION Considering the guidelines for self-development above, how have you applied any of them? What was the impact?

Leadership development for others

Leaders and managers have a major role in influencing the learning of their staff, by their own role modelling, by their support, and by coaching and mentoring as appropriate. They have a responsibility to develop and retain talent which can be especially demanding in the context of developing future leaders. A 'developmental leader' focuses on talent and how it can be developed; they become a coach themselves and develop their own skills in this arena. It is particularly important that leaders recognize potential in others, that they 'see people in terms of their future potential, not just past or present performance' (Kermally, 2004, 24). The tools for self-assessment are equally valid when supporting others' leadership development. The aim is to provide access to a range of tools and approaches and to provide a supportive environment and framework for discussions and feedback. Several authors see performance appraisal as a leadership development tool, providing opportunities to link corporate vision and objectives with the employee's performance objectives, and enabling feedback and reflection on development needs.

Many things can be done by managers to create and maintain a supportive climate for learning for developing leaders, for example:

1   Provide financial support for formal education and training such as a leadership programme.
2   Arrange a seminar series focusing on leadership from different perspectives.
3   Provide opportunities for job assignments or projects that help individuals test their leadership skills and develop new skills.
4   Establish a sabbatical programme so individuals can undertake research or some form of learning.
5   Provide awards for innovation and improvement.
6   Embody and encourage values such as experimentation, self-development, continuous learning and innovation.

REFLECTION Can you think of a manager who has created the right conditions for learning for you? What worked well?

Above all, managers can and should engage with their staff as individuals, understand their strengths, their ambitions, their fears and their potential, and spend time listening to them and supporting them. All managers therefore have the potential to act as coaches to their staff throughout their day-to-day relationships; as one manager explains, 'Being able to listen and ask the right questions, to understand a problem quickly and give positive feedback is what I see as my coaching responsibility' (Parsloe and Wray, 2000, 52). In addition, when individuals attend training and development – in whatever form, and whether formal or experiential – their manager can enable deeper learning. Figure 7.7 illustrates what can be done before and after the development 'event'.

Before the development event
Keep staff informed of training opportunities
Explain why the event would be beneficial
Change the work schedule to enable them to attend
Support preparation activities
Inform staff they will be asked to report back on what was learned and could be applied within the work place

After the event
Meet the member of staff to discuss what was learned and how it can be applied
Jointly set specific objectives and an action plan
Hold review sessions to monitor progress
Provide praise to reinforce the skills application
Provide encouragement and coaching when problems occur
Set an example by using the skills yourself

Figure 7.7 Ways to support leadership development in your staff

Towards a learning organization

A great deal has been written on organizational culture in relation to learning, with many authors seeing the development of a learning culture as vital to success and development. The concept of the *learning organization*, derived from Argyris and Schon (1996) and Senge (1990), supports the notion that work must become more 'learningful' at all levels. A learning organization is one that learns continuously to transform itself, where learning is context-ualized and occurs at all levels. Senge (1990) describes the learning organization as comprising five learning disciplines:

◆ *personal mastery* – aspiration, an understanding of what you as an individual wants to achieve
◆ *mental models* – reflection and enquiry, constant review, challenging assumptions
◆ *shared vision* – collective vision, commitment to common purpose and goals
◆ *team learning* – group interaction, collective thinking and action directed towards achievement of goals
◆ *systems thinking* – understanding interdependency and complexity, constant feedback for development.

Exploring this from another perspective, Bennis and Nanus (1997) explain how within a learning organization learning occurs at all levels:

◆ *individuals* – learn in their daily work, through their interactions with each other
◆ *groups* – learn as they co-operate to meet shared goals
◆ *the entire system* – learns as it obtains feedback from the environment and anticipates further changes.

Argyris and Schon's (1996) model of organizational learning introduces the concepts of single and double loop learning. Single loop learning is concerned with responding to changes in the environment without changing the core set of organizational norms; double loop learning occurs when organizations respond to changes in their environment by challenging and redefining underlying assumptions and organizational norms. Double loop learning is tightly coupled with the organization's ability to adapt its learning processes, or to control how it learns. It should be noted that other authors started to develop related concepts such as the learning laboratory, the knowledge-creating organization (Nonaka and Takeuchi, 1995), and the knowing organization. A recent contribution from Goh (2003) suggests that the building blocks of a learning organization are clarity of mission and vision, leadership commitment and empowerment, experimentation and rewards, effective transfer of knowledge, and teamwork and group problem solving.

How does the concept of the learning organization – and the need for library and information services to develop and foster such characteristics – support leadership development? How can leaders contribute to creating a learning organization? The effectiveness of any approach to leadership development and learning depends in part on the organizational conditions that facilitate or inhibit learning, and how this learning is then applied. Conger and Riggio are particularly critical of a leader development model based on leadership competencies and suggest an alternative model based on experiences: 'Leaders . . . are forged by the fires of experience: the assignments, people, challenges, and screw-ups that, over the course of a lifetime, push us beyond what we are' (2007, 89). They argue that organizations should be:

◆   identifying challenges not competencies
◆   identifying experiences, not programmes
◆   identifying people who can make the most of the experiences offered
◆   helping people to learn from the experiences they have.

Consequently, information services that aim to become 'learningful' and provide opportunities for learning at all levels can provide more fertile ground for potential leaders to develop. Leaders themselves have a key role in organizational learning; their very behaviour serves to direct and energize learning as they lead by example. They can redesign organizations to become more receptive to learning by becoming more open and participative. In the model of 21st-century leadership explored throughout this book, the leaders' role in learning development has shifted, from:

Leader as boss, controlling processes and behaviours	to	Leader as coach, enabling learning
Leader responsible for developing good managers	to	Leader responsible for developing future leaders; serving as leader of leaders

We wish to add a further dimension to this discussion around the learning organization that interlinks with the role of the leader: the connection between organizational learning and ethics. As we have emphasized elsewhere in this book, organizations are coming under increasing pressure not only to learn, change and adapt but to take actions that are ethically acceptable, and which balance the interests of a range of different stakeholders. In other words there are increasing expectations that organizations should act wisely or with wisdom. 'Good decisions' are not just short-term, goal-achieving decisions but ones that sustain the integrity of the organization based on the moral value of the organizational ethos. Leaders across an organization must instill these values and model them in their own practice and decision making.

Summary and conclusions

Undoubtedly, leadership is an 'educable enterprise' (Hernon, Powell and Young, 2003, 175) that requires constant and continuous commitment to learning and applying that learning to professional practice. The ability to learn and understand approaches to learning is a key quality of effective leaders both for themselves and for their colleagues. There are a variety of leadership learning approaches and experiences available to us, and each individual will respond differently at different stages in their careers and lives. Being aware of the choices available for ourselves and others, and how we might respond to these, is therefore vital. Within the library and information sector there have been significant developments in leadership programmes internationally which have had major impacts on participants. Other less formal and resource intensive approaches can also yield major results, in particular coaching and mentoring within and outside the organization, and experiential learning. Finally, within this chapter we explored the concept of the learning organization, and the argument that developing a conducive environment to learning – one that is open, challenging, no-blame, connected – is the most important action of a leader and the most critical to enabling other people's development within the organization. Oldroyd (2004) also stresses the importance of strategic planning for leadership development within library and information services. Just as each individual must take responsibility for their own learning and development, managers and the organization must provide the best learning environment. Factors to support the strategic planning for leadership development include the following:

1 Management and leadership development must be a key element of a library strategic plan.
2 There must be demonstrable commitment and resources to support staff in this.
3 Mentoring and coaching skills should be developed across the service.
4 The culture must be supportive of learning.
5 Managers should be role models, involved in lifelong learning themselves.
6 Managers should develop aspirations in others and recognize and foster potential in a wide range of staff.

Whether we are already in a senior leadership role, aspiring to leadership or leading from whatever level in the library context, we face significant challenges that at certain times can be overwhelming. Ongoing engagement and commitment to leadership development, using a range of tools and approaches, enables us to meet these challenges more effectively, while also helping to create optimum learning conditions for others.

Review questions

1 Explain the different elements of Kolb's learning cycle.
2 Define experiential learning. Why can it be a powerful learning tool for leadership development in library and information services?
3 What are the seven intelligences?
4 What are the main differences between coaching and mentoring? When would you use each one?
5 How would you summarize the main approaches adopted by LIS leadership programmes?
6 Why use a leadership self-assessment tool?
7 How can LIS managers provide a supportive climate for leadership learning?
8 What is a learning organization and how can a library become one?

Challenges

1 Is there an answer to the LIS 'leadership problem'? Is it leadership development programmes?

2 How can libraries best use the principles of experiential learning and embed them in everyday practices?

3 If coaching and mentoring are seen as addressing the deficiencies of traditional training, why bother with formal leadership training at all?

4 Should all LIS managers have to develop coaching skills?

5 Should leadership programmes for the library profession be sector specific and only for library professionals? If so, why?

6 Do you think that librarians prioritize leadership development?

7 When and why does leadership development fail to make an impact?

Case study interview with Deborah Dalley, Deborah Dalley and Associates Ltd, UK

Deborah Dalley has been working as a freelance consultant for over 20 years, primarily within the public sector. Client organizations include a number of county councils, 15 universities and colleges, libraries, NHS trusts, magistrates' courts and police forces. Her particular areas of expertise are:

- managing change and transition
- leadership development
- team coaching and team development
- organizational culture change
- 360 degree feedback.

Over the last few years much of her work has been focused around the challenges facing leaders in rapidly changing workplaces – much of this work has been with leaders from academic and public libraries. Research shows that leaders impact on organizational climate by up to 75% and organizational climate affects performance by up to 50%.

1 Tell us about your philosophy for developing leaders for the library and information sector.

My philosophy for developing leaders is summed up by the following quote 'Leadership in the future will be distributed among diverse individuals and teams who share responsibility for creating the organization's future' (Peter Senge). Today successful leadership focuses on gaining commitment from followers rather than compliance. The most effective leaders I have worked with explore ways to give power away rather than exerting it. They see their role as providing a vision, inspiring others, sharing information, acting as a role model and coaching. In many traditional library environments the culture of 'command and control' still exists. However, as the library and information sector has become more complex and technical this has become an increasingly difficult culture to sustain. There are very few, if any, senior managers who have the 'expert' knowledge necessary to control all parts of this rapidly developing arena. It is therefore essential that leadership is shared through empowerment: empowerment in the workplace must integrate key aspects of personal empowerment, responsibility, accountability and shared risk taking.

2 How would you summarize the leadership development needs of this sector?

Leadership is a process that can be learned and everyone has the potential to develop their performance above and beyond even their own expectations. Leadership development is, therefore, about a number of things:

- personal awareness – individuals need to understand themselves in order to effectively manage others; this includes exploring our values and recognizing the effect our past experience has on our outlook
- authenticity – leaders who know how to manage their authenticity will be more effective for it – it is key to recognize the impact we make on others
- understanding others and their motivation
- creating a culture of empowerment.

3 What methods have worked well for you and why? What hasn't worked as well as expected?

The most successful programmes I have been involved in have been where many different elements have been incorporated and the process has been seen as a long term initiative not a quick fix. Methods have included training sessions, facilitated meetings, personal learning logs, appraisal, coaching, etc. The least effective have been training courses that have been run without any real commitment to embedding the desired changes into the overall culture. It is very difficult for individuals to transfer anything back to work if the prevailing culture is working against what they are trying to do. This 'quick fix' approach is often taken by leaders who believe that the problems start 'below them' – a question I frequently get asked during middle management training sessions is 'Why aren't our senior managers here? Have they already done this?' and in many cases the truth is that they don't believe they need to. Where senior managers do not see themselves as part of the leadership development journey they become increasingly isolated from the views and concerns of their managers. This often results in them becoming distrustful about the motivation of those staff and they begin to hold on to power more tightly and eventually this fosters a culture of blame and dependency.

4   How have individuals responded to programmes/courses? Where have you seen high impact results and why do you think this happened?

During the time I have worked in the field of learning and development one thing that I have observed is often missing from leaders' development is the opportunity to receive high quality, in depth feedback. The further up an organization you go the harder it is to get feedback that does not come with some kind of agenda. I have found some of the highest impact work I have done has been providing ways for people to get that feedback. I have designed several 360 degree appraisal processes to gather feedback on leadership style and then helped leaders to develop personal action plans based on that feedback. I have also developed, in conjunction with a colleague, a series of workshops called 'The Beyond Series' that bring together small groups of people from diverse organizations and provide opportunity to receive feedback on presence, influence and impact. These have been extraordinarily powerful learning events.

5   What do you think are the key trends in the future of leadership development?

I believe that the future of leadership development lies in continuing to help find ways to distribute leadership throughout the organization. This will not be purely about running training courses but will be about the whole culture and will include:

- the vision, values and goals of the organization being shared, communicated and understood
- individual and team targets being set to align to the overall vision and goals
- a performance management system that rewards the right things and encourages talent
- development programmes that excite and challenge.

Coaching and mentoring are key parts of that picture as they enable individuals to realize their full potential.

References and additional reading

Argyris, C. and Schon, D. (eds) (1996) *Organisational Culture II: theory, method and practice*, Cambridge, MA, Addison-Wesley.

Armstrong, T. (1993) 7 *Kinds of Smart: identifying and developing your many intelligences*, New York, Plume.

Barbian, J. (2002) A Little Help From Your Friends: an employee with ample job knowledge and experience is a trainer waiting to happen, *Training*, **39** (3), 38.

Beard, C. and Wilson, J. P. (2002) *The Power of Experiential Learning*, London, Kogan Page.

Bennis, W. and Nanus, B. (1997) *Leaders: strategies for taking charge*, 2nd edn, London, HarperBusiness.

Brockmeyer, D. (2005) *Seeking Soul in Library Leadership*, Lanham, MD, Scarecrow Press.

Bruce, L. and Roberts, S. (2003) Shaping Tomorrow's Leaders Today: job shadowing as a professional development tool, *Library + Information Update*, September.

Conger, J. A. and Riggio, R. E. (eds) (2007) *The Practice of Leadership: developing the next generation of leaders*, San Francisco, Jossey-Bass Inc.

Frye Leadership Institute (n.d.), www.fryeinstitute.org/.

Goh, S. C. (2003) Improving Organizational Learning Capability: lessons for two case studies, *Learning Organization*, **10** (4), 216–27.

Harvard Business Review (2004) *Harvard Business Review on Developing Leaders*, Boston, Harvard Business School Publishing.

Hernon, P., Powell, R. R. and Young, A. P. (2003) *The Next Library Leadership: attributes of academic and public library directors*, Westport, Libraries Unlimited.

Holden, R. and McGrath, J. (1992) Shadowing for Self Development, *Journal of Further and Higher Education*, **16** (2), (Summer), 40–9.

Honey, P. and Mumford, A. (1982) *Manual of Learning Styles*, Maidenhead, Peter Honey Publishing.

Kermally, S. (2004) *Developing and Managing Talent: a blueprint for business survival*, London, Thorogood.

Kolb, D. (1984) *Experiential Learning: experience as the source of learning and development*, London, Prentice-Hall.

Nonaka, I. and Takeuchi, H. (1995) *The Knowledge Creating Company*, Oxford, Oxford University Press.

Oldroyd, M. (ed.) (2004) *Developing Academic Library Staff for Future Success*, London, Facet Publishing.

Parsloe, E. and Wray, M. (2000) *Coaching and Mentoring: practical methods to improve learning*, London, Kogan Page.

Rigg, S. and Richards, S. (eds) (2006) *Action Learning, Leadership and Organisational Development in Public Services*, London, Routledge.

Ritchie, A. and Walker, C. (2007) (eds) *Continuing Professional Development: pathways to leadership in the library and information world*, IFLA Publications 126, Munich, K. G. Saur.

Senge, P. (1990) *The Fifth Discipline: the art and practice of the learning organisation*, New York, Doubleday Currency.

Shakespeare, J. (1994) Work shadowing, *Training Officer*, **30** (3), (April), 80–1.

Stevenson, V. (2006) Future Leaders Programme, March 2006–2007, *SCONUL Focus*, **37**, (Spring).

Yukl, G. (2002) *Leadership in Organisations*, 5th edn, New Jersey, Prentice Hall.

Influential leadership

Learning objectives

After reading this chapter you should be able to:

☑ understand the information professional's value beyond the library
context
☑ appreciate approaches and issues related to working with politics and
power
☑ reflect on the influence of library and information professionals within
wider contexts
☑ consider two specific case studies that illustrate influential leadership
☑ consider the importance of developing a 'leading organization' as well
as leading individuals.

Introduction

Chapter 8 explores the role of the information professional in leading and
influencing in contexts beyond the library, where the other stakeholders are
not information professionals. We feel this is of particular importance in
today's organizations where libraries and library and information professionals
are often working – and indeed are expected to work – beyond traditional

boundaries and in doing so can provide added value. This blurring of boundaries brings multiple opportunities for wider influence and greater impact, but clearly requires a high level of influential leadership. This involves understanding and capitalizing on the leadership, management and information competences that working in an information service or information industry environment develops. This chapter thus begins with a discussion of the value of the information professional beyond the library context and explores specific examples of leadership and influence. We then focus on issues related to working with politics and power, and leadership approaches to them. This final chapter is different from the others in the book as it provides two detailed case studies to illustrate leadership and influence where library and information professionals have made significant impact both within and beyond organizations. These examples are drawn from real life experiences from different sectors – health and higher education. They also provide insights into the individuals who influenced within these contexts. Consequently, the chapter does not include a case cameo interview. We conclude with reflecting on the relationship between developing influential leadership at an individual level and developing leading organizations.

Leadership and influence

The theme of influential leadership has pervaded this book. Leaders at all levels use their influence to lead and motivate people, to implement change, to lead teams and to shape values and culture. We have provided diverse examples of this influence in practice throughout each chapter. Many authors write about 'influencing skills' and suggest that we can simply learn these skills in order to manage and lead people effectively. Although we can definitely develop and perfect our skills of communication and impression management (see Chapter 2) we would argue that true and extensive influence stems from authenticity and congruence and cannot be simply reduced to a competencies based approach. The literature on influencing often focuses on techniques that require you to be a kind of chameleon rather than showing your inner values, qualities and beliefs.

Leaders who act with authenticity and congruence understand themselves and behave accordingly. Burton and Dalley (2007) summarize the 'art of influencing' in the following way:

◆ an understanding of who you are and what you stand for
◆ congruence and authenticity (the link between our identity and values and the behaviour we exhibit generates trust)
◆ empathy with others
◆ communication capability (questioning, listening, feedback)
◆ intent (most successful influencers are those who operate from values such as truth, trust and integrity)
◆ ease with uncertainty
◆ ease with interdependence.

Conceptualizing influence in this way is challenging as it does not provide 'easy answers' or techniques but begins with self-exploration and questioning, so 'the work is from the inside out – develop yourself and you develop your world' (Burton and Dalley, 2007).

REFLECTION How would you assess yourself against the seven skills needed to be successful at influencing, highlighted above?

Compare this model based on authenticity and congruence with a second model of influencing which neatly encapsulates the range of tactics available to leaders. This is summarized in Table 8.1.

Table 8.1 Influencing tactics available to leaders (Yukl, 2002)

Rational persuasion	Logical arguments, facts and figures in support of particular objectives
Inspirational appeals	Focus on values, ideals, aspirations
Consultation	Participation, willingness to adjust a viewpoint or approach
Ingratiation	Praise, flattery, friendship
Personal appeals	Calling on loyalty, friendship
Exchange	Offers of reciprocation or sharing benefits to meet joint objectives
Coalition tactics	Seeking the aid of others to exercise persuasion
Pressure	Demands, threats, constant checking or reminders
Legitimating tactics	Claiming authority, verifying a request in line with organizational policy

As Yukl makes clear, it is important to use the right tactics in the right circumstances. We agree that being aware of different approaches, and understanding what could work in different contexts, can be valid and valuable. However, in comparison with beginning with personal authenticity and congruence, the tactics approach could appear manipulative and shallow.

REFLECTION Can you identify times when you have seen leaders use the influencing tactics listed in Table 8.1? What influence did they have?

The information professional's value beyond the library

In researching and writing this book, and our previous book *Managing Information Services* (Roberts and Rowley, 2003), we have been overwhelmed by the diversity of library and information services, the multiplicity of management and leadership roles, and their wide-ranging impact. We have aimed to demonstrate this in part through the examples we have used throughout the book. The value of the information profession in general is effectively articulated by the professional bodies who are also reflecting changes in roles. Consider the following information from CILIP (UK) and the American Library Association and how they represent the value of information professionals:

> The information professional's role has changed significantly. Many traditional information roles no longer have the term 'library' or 'librarian' in their job title. There has been a growth in electronic and digital libraries. You may see the following job titles in job adverts:
>
> • information manager
> • internet librarian
> • knowledge assistant
> • learning advisor
> • web developer.
>
> (CILIP, n.d.)

> **Make a living making a difference . . .**
> Consider joining the 400,000 librarians and library workers who bring opportunity every day to the communities they serve.
>
> (American Library Association, n.d.)

The value of information professionals to an organization – and to society in general – extends, we believe, beyond the management and leadership of the library or information service. This wider influence can in part be attributed to the professional values and ethics that underpin and guide the work of library and information staff. It can be argued that the library and information profession has a particular set of values that are common across sectors and organizational types. A common set of information professional values could be said to include belief in:

◆ the value of information
◆ accessibility to information, services and support
◆ customer focus
◆ social inclusion.

CILIP's ethical principles for library and information professionals (published in 2007 and depicted in Figure 8.1) expand on these values and further indicate how individuals who work to these principles can influence their organization. For example, library professionals who believe in promoting equal opportunities would take a lead in equity initiatives, acting as a catalyst and influencing other departments within the organization to get involved in projects.

REFLECTION Do you feel that CILIP's ethical principles should underpin library and information practice? Why or why not?

In addition to understanding how these values can influence organizations we must also understand and capitalize on the leadership, management and information competences that working in an information service or information industry environment develops. These will undoubtedly vary depending on the context; however, in general information professionals will be influential if they:

◆ understand user communities and are able to create and tailor services and information to those communities
◆ are effective managers of resources
◆ are information seekers and assessors – crucial in a knowledge economy that depends on the sifting and interpretation of information

The conduct of members should be characterized by the following general principles, presented here in no particular order of priority:

- concern for the public good in all professional matters, including respect for diversity within society, and the promoting of equal opportunities and human rights
- concern for the good reputation of the information profession
- commitment to the defence, and the advancement, of access to information, ideas and works of the imagination
- provision of the best possible service within available resources
- concern for balancing the needs of actual and potential users and the reasonable demands of employers
- equitable treatment of all information users
- impartiality, and avoidance of inappropriate bias, in acquiring and evaluating information and in mediating it to other information users
- respect for confidentiality and privacy in dealing with information users
- concern for the conservation and preservation of our information heritage in all formats
- respect for, and understanding of, the integrity of information items and for the intellectual effort of those who created them
- commitment to maintaining and improving personal professional knowledge, skills and competences
- respect for the skills and competences of all others, whether information professionals or information users, employers or colleagues.

Figure 8.1 CILIP's ethical principles for library and information professionals

◆ are customer service orientated – within a larger organization information services will often be one of the most customer-facing
◆ build relationships with their stakeholders
◆ are focused on quality enhancement
◆ are often viewed by others as contributing to the 'common good'.

In order to maximize the values and competencies illustrated above, several authors have stressed the need for information professionals to act as 'enabling partners' – traversing the silos of an organization to bring different groups together. They should also act in a more entrepreneurial way, seeking out ways in which to add value and make significant contributions to the organization's goals that go beyond the traditional parameters of an information service. Bundy tells us to go beyond the 'self-limited role focused just on information identification' (2003). The two case studies in this chapter describe in detail how different library and information services, and the individuals involved, have taken on a wider leadership role to influence their organizations to change or influence wider communities. Before exploring these case studies it would be useful to provide a range of examples where library and information professionals have influenced their organization, and also where they have taken on broader portfolios of responsibility as a result. We would categorize these as:

◆ leadership of converged information services within education contexts that comprise libraries and a range of other related services, for example IT, student skills support, media services; the aim is often to provide an integrated experience for staff and students and a one-stop-shop approach to learning services; for example see Hanson (2005)
◆ information professionals within different contexts who have taken on extended responsibilities for knowledge management and information management; as Hart (2007) says, 'Evolution of the information professional role requires a knowledge of content and an understanding of how technology can help differentiate your organization'
◆ public librarians who have championed quality improvement processes and customer feedback strategies that have been extended to other public services or have worked in partnership with other services to provide a unified approach for customers
◆ individual library and information professionals who have become champions for particular issues that have wide ranging influence; for example the open scholarship movement, which encourages web publishing by academics to make research more accessible.

REFLECTION Can you think of other examples where information professionals have influenced their organization and taken on broader roles?

It is also important to reflect on why this wider influence has occurred; what factors could have contributed to the examples provided above? We would suggest that the individuals involved focused on their organization's business strategy and priorities and how they could add value to them; they were skilled in particular areas and transferred these skills to other contexts, for example providing excellent management of other library-related teams; they made connections between different services and took a holistic and strategic approach; they were highly effective networkers who made alliances and worked collaboratively to make a difference; and they had the customers' needs as their priority and aimed to meet them by looking at the bigger picture.

Working with politics and power

'The political role of the information service manager is to make things happen' (Bryson, 2006, 119). In order to influence, leaders at any level – not just managers – must know how to get things done within their organization and know how to use power constructively. Skilled political leaders understand what the organization wants and how they and their service and staff can create solutions to the problems facing the organization. Consequently, leaders must interpret the political environment correctly, identify supporters, build networks and gain commitment. In this section we will explore the different elements of working with power and politics, beginning with French and Raven's (Bryson, 1990) model of power bases, illustrated in Table 8.2.

Table 8.2 Bases of power

Position power	Reward power	Being able to grant favours or benefits
	Coercive power	Through punishment, threats or control
	Legitimate power	Through authority or your status/role
Personal power	Expert power	Through your skills and competencies
	Referent power	Through being attractive to someone else who wishes to please you

REFLECTION Thinking of a leader you have worked with, can you identify when they have used different bases of power?

Leaders must be aware of the different bases of power and use them appropriately and ethically. As Adair emphasizes, 'Leadership is the intelligent and sensitive use of power' (2003, 157) and within the context of modern leadership there is a strong emphasis upon developing and enabling the power of others through participative leadership and empowerment. Yukl (2002) also stresses that 'researchers have begun to examine the specific types of behaviour used to exercise influence, rather than focus exclusively on power as a source of potential influence'. Undoubtedly, the concept and model of power expressed in Table 8.2 is shifting as notions of leadership change. This links back to our previous discussion around influencing tactics and authenticity.

Our ability to influence remains closely linked to how we engage with organizational politics, which has been defined as the ways in which individuals 'acquire, develop, and use power and other resources to obtain one's outcome in a situation' (Bryson, 1990, 251). Research on library leadership by Pors and Johannsen (2003) highlighted political action on the part of the senior leader as central and stressed the role of the director:

◆ who has to make the library visible in the political system
◆ whose political legitimacy will be very important
◆ who must create political contacts and networks.

We would stress the need for staff at other levels to be aware of the political context and to work on all three of the above, for example developing their own networks within and beyond the organization. The political positioning of the library and information service should also not be the end in itself but should be motivated by the desire to enhance services to customers and for the good of the organization as a whole. Table 8.3 lists ethical and unethical political tactics that can be used in organizations. We would argue once again that if a leader is authentic and congruent in their approach – and has a clear intent that is focused upon achieving the goals of the organization – they will be in a positive position to influence without it appearing that they are 'empire building' or focused on personal agendas. In the context of the need for increased partnerships both within organizations – between libraries and other

Table 8.3 Ethical and unethical political tactics (after Bryson, 2006)

Clean tactics (ethical)	Dirty tactics (unethical)
Establishing an alliance with others who are willing to support the preferred position or action	Attacking or blaming others
Choosing a powerful mentor	Deliberately misleading others
Developing a base of support for one's ideas	Using hidden agendas
Creating obligations and a basis for reciprocity	

areas such as information technology, research, education and training – and externally across libraries to maximize access and resources, library leaders must be expert and ethical influencers and negotiators.

The development of networks is viewed as a key strategy in influential leadership. 'Networking' can – unjustly we feel – be seen as superficial, manipulative and something that people don't really want to do! But a network is broadly speaking a natural coalition, a group with joint interests. There are various types of networks, which can be categorized as:

◆ *Practician-oriented networks* – individuals who have similar expertise, training or professional interests; they provide intellectual and professional support and a supportive environment for new ideas.
◆ *Power networks* – individuals who have (or wish to have) substantial influence; these groups work through personal power bases and can be very closed.
◆ *Ideological networks* – individuals who wish to pursue a particular idea, for example technology enthusiasts.
◆ *People-oriented networks* – these exist purely for the sake of their members and provide information and support.

Networking as an activity can be viewed differently from 'networks' as described above. Individuals can be members of various types of networks but can also undertake 'networking' across the organization. Colley (2007) explains the reasons for information professionals to be involved in networking from the perspective of a business context:

◆ to influence the right stakeholders
◆ to market your department and staff
◆ to build a business case
◆ to communicate change in the right way
◆ to gain a strategic overview of the business
◆ to identify strategic goals and continually realign the information service
◆ to go after new business and reposition the information service
◆ to build partnerships with other business units
◆ to spot the drivers for change in your company.

All these reasons could be applied to any library and information context and reinforce the importance of personal connectedness and of collaboration in order to be an influential leader.

REFLECTION What are your thoughts on networks and networking? Can you identify opportunities for extending your own networks?

Case studies

The two case studies below illustrate ways in which library and information professionals have significantly influenced their organizations and wider communities. They are deliberately drawn from dissimilar contexts to demonstrate what influential leadership can achieve in very different circumstances. The leaders involved have written some parts of their own case studies and we gratefully acknowledge their contributions.

Case Study 1: Learning support and learning environments (higher education libraries), University of Cumbria, UK - The Learning Gateway
Margaret Weaver, Head of Learning and Information Services

Context

The University of Cumbria was formed on 1 August 2007 from the amalgamation of St Martin's College, Cumbria Institute of the Arts and the Cumbria campuses of the University of Central Lancashire. It has 15,000 students studying mainly vocational subjects in education, health, arts, natural resources and social sciences, spread across seven sites in Cumbria, North Lancashire, and London. The University is committed to widening access to higher education across the generations. The University's academic strategy is predicated on the belief that students will only flourish if their learning experience is active, has meaning for them and gives them 21st-century skills for changing lifestyles and workplaces. The University's plan was a holistic one – to invest in its learning environment and create a new kind of learning space – the Learning Gateway – at its Fusehill campus in Carlisle. Leadership of this project was undertaken by the Head of Learning and Information Services and her team.

What has been achieved?

The Learning Gateway opened in April 2006 and can support up to 500 people. It combines formal and informal learning spaces, a 150-seat lecture theatre, and wireless technology. The Learning Gateway concept is based on the assumption that the relationship between the physical setting and the students' learning experience is vital and that the latter can be enhanced if the former is designed right from the start. A set of pedagogical principles informed the build, the furnishings, the technology and the services. Every decision about the form and function of the space was made using constructivist learning approaches in the belief that these best inspire active learning.

Flexibility is at the heart of the Learning Gateway so that the space has something to offer everyone – students, tutors and visitors. A new learning facilitation team in the Gateway integrates the roles of IT support, learning advice and library assistance. The Gateway has also spawned a new team-working concept in the University; it is being used to describe academic support made up from different service staff, assisting tutors to develop their teaching practice.

Influential leadership: Margaret Weaver

As Head of Learning and Information Services (LIS) at the University of Cumbria, Margaret is responsible for Library, IT User Support, Media and Learning Technology Services. She is the strategic lead of the Learning Gateway and the Change Academy team – a national programme for top change managers sponsored by the UK Higher Education Academy. She has worked in a number of north west universities and written various articles on learning and teaching support within a HE setting.

Margaret reflects on the impact of the Learning Gateway, her leadership role and what she has learned, in her own words:

> I hope this case study shows that the Learning Gateway was a step change for the University; it is significant that a librarian was the leader of this project rather than the Head of Estates, who would normally lead new builds. Throughout the project I had to persuade and explain that the Learning Gateway had a different intention to traditional teaching space; not everyone understood this at first. I think the Change Academy work that ran alongside was helpful and having a

leadership role in both projects diffused more knowledge across the institution.

The vision for the Learning Gateway was sponsored by a member of the Senior Executive (essential to gain support for what were quite radical ideas in 2004). With an unforseen change in the executive team after the project was completed came the need to restate and refresh the strategic nature of the Learning Gateway and to emphasize its benefit to the University.

Securing the support of other departments especially the faculties and relevant services is essential. I made sure that the Learning Gateway was discussed at University committees and embedded in the new Learning and Teaching Strategy. Communicating for multiple audiences involved understanding their motivations and being able to paint a vivid picture. Also having enthusiasm for the project yourself helps others to feel confident in your specific contribution. I also undertook research into learning spaces internationally to get a grasp of what others were doing. At the end of the day, though, no one tells you the 'answer'. You have to decide what is right for your institution and have the courage of your convictions.

You need to be aware of how your decisions will be interpreted by your stakeholder groups. If time had allowed I would have consulted more with students although students were on the steering group. For example, whilst we thought carefully about the terminology for the space – devising new words to denote usage such as 'flexi-room' and 'community spaces' – maybe students would have chosen differently? I don't think you are necessarily looking for consensus but as a leader you have to be prepared to instigate these debates and listen to them.

On reflection, having an excellent team around you is essential and being prepared to let your creativity flow together is important. As a leader, you have to make difficult decisions, mitigate risks and live with uncertainty. In this project, for example, it was not certain that tutors would use the space as intended and the tension between flexibility and intuitive use of space and space utilization is an ongoing debate.

Wider themes and influence: what has this project meant to the University and to the sector?

The Learning Gateway has become a flagship for the University and also an exciting place for innovation in learning. There have been conferences and events, not originally envisaged, that have brought the University closer to its community. This has meant that prospective students have seen a very positive view of the University and its commitment to students. It has connected a range of learners via technology, which a distributed institution must surely embrace, such as video conferencing with schools and further education colleges.

There have been many visitors to the space from other institutions wishing to implement similar innovations and the Gateway has hosted national conferences on relevant themes. The Joint Information Systems Committee has recognized the University's vision by accepting the Learning Gateway for the national JISC info kit (www.jiscinfonet.ac.uk/infokits/learning-space-design/more/case-studies/smc/success).

A recent e-mail survey of staff and students showed that the space is having a positive impact:

1 Flexibility and convenience was appreciated by tutors and students especially in relation to interaction and the ability to move from individual to group learning situations (and back again) easily and freely.
2 The impact that the space had on students was felt to be significant for example helping them to feel relaxed and ready to learn, promoting learning between formal and informal situations and at home.
3 Tutor perspectives as teachers demonstrated that the space was affording experimentation that could not be found elsewhere on campus.

Finally it demonstrates the potential of library professionals to transform learner support services, so that library staff are not seen as static, but as a connective team of experts able to blend technology, space and facilitation – with amazing results!

Further information

University of Cumbria, www.cumbria.ac.uk
Learning Gateway, www.cumbria.ac.uk/Services/lis/learninggateway/home.aspx

Case study 2: Clinical information skills (health libraries), Aintree University Hospital, UK – Clinical Information Service
Rachel Bury and Michelle Maden

Context

Information needs are becoming ever more complex and central to our working and personal lives: no more so than in the National Health Service (NHS) in the UK. The Library and Information Resource Centre (LIRC) at Aintree University Hospital, Liverpool, aims to provide support services and facilities to help NHS users successfully manage professional commitments and continuing development. The LIRC is managed and led by Edge Hill University's Learning Services and provides a rich resource for the University's NHS partners. The core of that support over the past two years has been based around the Clinical Information Service.

The LIRC is not simply a physical learning centre but a resource which has had an impact on the NHS users, partnerships and the strategic development of those involved. This case study illustrates how leadership and collaboration outside the library has impacted on staff and users across all the partner organizations, particularly in the development of NHS staff skills and approaches. It illustrates how libraries saw an opportunity (nationally and locally) to make a difference to NHS staff training in the context of national initiatives to develop health practitioners.

What has been achieved?

The clinical information specialist supports the information needs of NHS partners across two acute NHS trusts and a primary care NHS trust, aiming to provide a flexible, proactive and responsive Clinical Information Service. The main focus of the role is:

- promoting a mediated literature search service to provide healthcare professionals with the evidence they require to support patient care
- designing and delivering information skills and critical appraisal skills training
- providing an outreach service to allow 'access for all'.

Delivering information to the point of healthcare needs is one of the biggest challenges facing information professions working within the ever changing environment of the NHS. The UK government is keen to ensure that all healthcare practices are evidence-based, in other words, healthcare practitioners are delivering patient care in a manner that is supported by quality research. This places information professionals in a unique position to enable busy NHS staff in their day-to-day decision making regarding patient care.

The evaluation of the service was a key component of the two-year project. The results from this evaluation have provided the key stakeholders with full validation and demonstrated the impact the service has had on those who have accessed support. The evaluation was undertaken to examine the uptake and to determine the value and impact of the service on healthcare professionals' own working practices and ultimately on improving patient care. Questionnaires and interviews using the critical incident technique provided specific examples of how the service actually made a difference to working practice. Respondents emphasized the improvement in their skills, the time-saving nature provided by the service and the added value the service provided above what they might have done themselves. The evaluation showed that people are using the information or skills provided by the service not only to support their own research, but also to answer questions relating to patient care, to develop guidelines and care pathways, and to aid in writing for publication or presenting at conferences.

Influential leadership: Rachel Bury and Michelle Maden

Rachel has been a library and information manager working in the field of health information for over 14 years. Rachel was very closely involved in the formation of the multidisciplinary service at the LIRC. More recently the role of the LIRC and the support it provides has shifted into strategic management of partnerships with the NHS and roles which are beyond the LIRC.

Michelle began her professional career in the NHS as an information officer supporting the information needs of an evidence-based emergency medicine research group. Michelle was appointed as a clinical information specialist in 2005. Initially started as a two-year project, the post is now permanent. Michelle is an active member of various North-West health librarian groups, supports the training needs of regional health librarians and has published articles on information retrieval techniques for locating health research in the professional literature.

Rachel's role in the initial phases of the project was one of championing the concept of the clinical information specialist and making a business case to fund the two-year pilot. A key theme from the planning stages was around demonstrating the impact the role could have and the risk involved in not moving forward with such service. Outlining advantages for all partners became the key message; however, with considerable costs involved for the NHS, this was challenging. The most important strategy employed when meeting key stakeholders was demonstrating impact, risk (what would happen if the project didn't happen) and value for money.

Michelle's role has been one of promoter, trainer, mentor and leader. An example of the extension of the role is mentoring and supporting those staff in the NHS involved in producing national guidelines. The emphasis on promotion focuses more on demonstrating *how* to make an impact rather than simply outlining *what* resources are available. Being aware of national initiatives can help raise the profile of the service. For example, linking the training on offer with the national NHS Knowledge and Skills Framework and competencies which NHS staff are required to demonstrate in order to progress through their pay scales increased the relevance and importance of the need for information skills and critical appraisal training.

Real-life examples taken from the service evaluation provide a powerful message in promoting the service to potential new users and senior NHS staff involved in training and development. Michelle works closely with the strategic lead of workforce development in the primary care trust and has been influential in ensuring information skills are at the top of the training agenda.

It is recognized that users cannot always physically access the service, therefore a flexible outreach approach has been adopted. Since the service crosses the traditional boundary of a physical library service to an outreach service, effective communication and influencing skills are essential. Michelle actively seeks out associations with new users to increase awareness of the service. Identifying library 'champions' to help promote the service enables targeted promotion of the service to people when an information need is first identified. For example, the clinical governance and research and development leads actively promote the service whenever researchers first register their research proposal.

The initial project, and subsequent development and establishment of the service, has brought new areas of collaboration, increased externality and a much greater understanding of the impact of our services. It is very rewarding to have evidence which now supports our initial proposal of why Aintree LIRC should provide a clinical information service.

Wider themes

The service works closely with regional health care librarians in sharing good practice and expertise in areas that cross the boundaries of higher education and the NHS. For example, facilitating critical appraisal workshops for library trainers across the north west and using emerging technologies (e.g. blogs) to disseminate information to the user at the point of need. The team has also presented on the topic of clinical information skills and services, influencing the wider community of both information professionals and health professionals.

Further information

Library blog, http://aintreelirc.blogspot.com
CIS blog, http://clinicalinformationspecialist.blogspot.com

REFLECTION What do the two case studies tell us about the leadership potential of information professionals? How did each individual involved influence wider stakeholder groups to ensure the success of their initiatives?

The leading organization

Elsewhere in this book we have explored the concept of the learning organization and the imperative for leaders to help develop a conducive environment for learning at all levels. The learning organization, we also argued, must base its decision making on ethical principles and not in a value-free vacuum. We wish to conclude this final chapter by making the link between individual leaders and the development of 'leading organizations'. Individual leaders who are transformational as opposed to transactional can help to create learning organizations; through empowerment and participative leadership they can help create 'leadership for all' and at all levels (Walton, 2007). In doing this, we would argue, library and information organizations have the potential to become 'leading organizations'. By this we mean organizations that influence the library profession, within and across sectors, and that can also influence beyond the library context. Such organizations aspire to continuous learning and transformation, they are viewed by others as exemplars in particular practices and are often held up as the benchmark for excellence. A leading organization that has leadership for all is also not ultimately dependent on specific individuals and has in-built capacity to ensure it will provide ongoing leadership in the future.

REFLECTION Can you identify a library and information service or body that you feel has the characteristics of a 'leading organization'?

Summary and conclusions

Library and information professionals and their organizations have the potential to influence across boundaries. We have explored in this chapter approaches to influencing, arguing that while influencing skills and tactics can be developed and employed effectively, the art of true influencing begins with authenticity and behaving congruently and ethically. Ethical approaches to decision making are particularly important and resonate with library and information associations' views on the value of the information profession. Power and politics have been described here as necessary in order to position the library service and to ensure that it enables the organization to meet its strategic goals. Leaders at all levels must engage in the politics of their organizations and service positively and effectively, rather than allowing politics and bureaucracy to stifle leadership and innovation (Van Nort, 2003). Networks – in their diverse forms – and networking are also seen as valuable concepts for the library leader throughout their career and can extend their sphere of influence and support mechanisms.

We hope that our two case studies have illustrated how different library and information services and professionals have taken influential leadership roles and in doing so how they have contributed significantly to the development of other professions, to the strategic direction of their wider organization and to the sector, and to national initiatives. They demonstrate what can be achieved by leadership that recognizes opportunities for libraries to move beyond traditional boundaries while also transferring key library skills and values. We end this chapter and the book with a challenge: as individual leaders our ultimate task is to aspire to create leading organizations. We hope that this book, with its integration of theory and practice, has provided you with frameworks and tools to apply to your own contexts, and, more importantly, has inspired and motivated you on your leadership journey.

Review questions

1 What are the seven key steps in the art of influencing?
2 How would you describe tactics for influencing?
3 What are the library and information profession's underpinning values?
4 How can the profession's ability to influence beyond the library be summarized?
5 What are the different bases of power?
6 Why are networks and networking important in developing influence in organizations and beyond?
7 How would you describe a leading organization?

Challenges

1 If influential leadership begins 'from the inside out' can influencing skills not be learnt and developed?
2 Should library and information professionals really have a leadership role beyond the library or will this merely detract from their core work?
3 Are CILIP's ethical principles realistic in the 21st century? Do information professionals work with these principles at the heart of their professional practice?
4 Why do you think power and politics are often viewed with scepticism? How can we ensure they are used positively and ethically?
5 Are library and information professionals good networkers? How could we be more effective in this?
6 What do the three case studies tell us about the challenges of leading beyond the library? What does this mean for library and information roles and professional practice?

References and additional reading

Adair, J. (2003) *Not Bosses but Leaders*, 3rd edn, with P. Reed, London, Kogan Page.
American Library Association, (n.d.)
www.ala.org/ala/education/educationcareers.htm.

Bryson, J. (1990) *Effective Library and Information Centre Management*, Aldershot, Gower.

Bryson, J. (2006) *Managing Information Services: a transformational approach*, 2nd edn, Aldershot, Ashgate.

Bundy, A. (2003) A Window of Opportunity: libraries and higher education, *Library Management*, **24** (8/9), 393–400.

Burton, L. and Dalley, B. (2007) *Beyond Influencing*, leadership seminar, Manchester.

CILIP (n.d.), www.cilip.org.uk/jobscareers/careeradvice/choose.

Colley, A. (2007) Business Contacts: the importance of internal networking, *Library + Information Update*, **6** (7–8), 28–31.

Hanson, T. (2005) (ed.) *Managing Academic Support Services in Universities: the convergence experience*, London, Facet Publishing.

Hart, C. (2007) Take Opportunities to Get Ahead, says Hart, *Library + Information Gazette*, (18–31 May), 1–2.

Pors, N. O. and Johannsen, C. G. (2003) Library Directors Under Cross-pressure between New Public Management and Value-based Management, *Library Management*, **24** (1/2), 51–60.

Roberts, S. and Rowley, J. (2003) *Managing Information Services*, London, Facet Publishing.

Van Nort, M. (2003) Public Sector Leadership: an assessment, *Public Administration Review*, **63** (2), 214–28.

Walton, G. (2007) Developing the Concepts of 'Leadership for All' in Library and Information Services. In Ritchie, A. and Walker, C. (eds), *Continuing Professional Development: pathways to leadership in the library and information world*, IFLA Publications 126, Munich, K. G. Saur.

Yukl, G. (2002) *Leadership in Organisations*, 5th edn, New Jersey, Prentice Hall.

Index